MAINSTREAMING CHILDREN
with Special Needs

MAINSTREAMING CHILDREN
with Special Needs

VERNA HART
University of Pittsburgh

Longman
New York & London

MAINSTREAMING CHILDREN WITH SPECIAL NEEDS

Longman Inc., 19 West 44th Street, New York, N.Y. 10036
Associated companies, branches, and representatives
throughout the world.

Copyright © 1981 by Longman Inc.

Developmental Editor: Lane Akers
Editorial and Design Supervisor: Diane Perlmuth
Interior Design: Pencils Portfolio, Inc.
Manufacturing and Production Supervisor: Maria Chiarino
Composition: Book Composition Services, Inc.
Printing and Binding: The Hunter Rose Company Ltd.
Cover Printed in U.S.A.

Figure 12.3. The Northampton (Yale) Chart, on page 123, adapted
from Caroline A. Yale, *Formation and Development of
Elementary English Sounds,* The Clarke School for the Deaf,
Northampton, Massachusetts, 1925. Reprinted by permission
of the publisher.

Library of Congress Cataloging in Publication Data

Hart, Verna.
   Mainstreaming children with special needs.

   Bibliography: p.
   Includes index.
   1. Handicapped children—Education. 2. Mainstreaming
in education. I. Title.
LC4019.H38   371.9   80-16297
ISBN 0-582-28211-X

Manufactured in Canada
9 8 7 6 5 4 3 2 1

To Helen Smith,
who mainstreamed a loved one
before the term was known

Contents

MAINSTREAMING CHILDREN
with Special Needs

Lift the film of handicap from your eyes
and see the person—the person who can learn,
the person who will thrill
to the joy of knowledge and truth.

PART 1
WHAT IS MAINSTREAMING?

You have just found out that you are to have a mainstreamed handicapped child in your classroom. You know that "mainstreaming" means taking handicapped children out of a special classroom for exceptional children and putting them in the regular class. However, you're really worried, because you know practically nothing about handicapped children. You try to remember your last contact with a handicapped child and what that child was like. Your cousin's baby was said to be "developmentally delayed," but he was so little the last time you saw him that you really couldn't tell how different from normal babies he was. When you were young the man down the street had a hearing loss, but you don't remember him being too different from the other men on the block. One of your friends had a sister who wore a brace on her leg, but she seemed pretty much like the other children in the family.

You finally decide that your experience with handicapping conditions is pretty limited, and that your educational experience and real knowledge of handicapped children is nonexistent. You become even more worried and fearful. What will you do with this child you know nothing about when he or she enters your classroom? You consider yourself a good teacher. Will this child ruin your self-concept as a teacher? Will you fail? Who can you go to with questions? Who can support you in your efforts to do a good job?

Your mind races. Why you? What is this mainstreaming thing, anyway? Why aren't handicapped children taught at schools for exceptional children the way they used to be? What is this law that says these children will be placed in regular classrooms? How did this happen?

This book is an attempt to help those of you who are now, or will be, teaching handicapped children within the regular classroom. Eventually, all teachers in regular classrooms may be teaching handicapped children at least part of every day. Mainstreaming did not happen overnight. It has had a long history with many events leading to the current situation of placing handicapped children within the regular classroom.

CHAPTER 1
HISTORICAL ANTECEDENTS

Throughout the history of civilization, handicapped children have received many different kinds of treatment. Long ago in some societies, but still a practice in others, handicapped children were allowed to die as infants. If those attending the birth noticed that there was an abnormality in the new-born child, often one of those present would smother the baby as soon after birth as possible, telling the mother that the child had either been stillborn or had not survived the rigors of childbirth. Some societies exposed afflicted children to the elements, while others abandoned them to the animals. Others would keep the children but would give them no attention, allowing them to die slowly.

It is difficult to imagine, but even today this is true in some of the world's less developed areas. For example, when the topic of education of the severely handicapped was discussed at a recent international confer- ence, several African delegates announced that such children didn't exist in their countries and therefore created no problem. Their concern was provid- ing education to nonhandicapped children, for development in their coun- tries was such that education in general was lacking for most segments of the population.

Historically, the spread of the Judeo-Christian philosophy, with its re- spect for human life, whether disabled or not, has had a great impact on handicapped individuals throughout the world. Because of that impact, even though this respect for life often faltered, those born handicapped or who became disabled later in life were sheltered and protected from those who would do them bodily harm. Many handicapped children were placed in asylums, protected and safe from those in the world who would be cruel to them. Mother Theresa, the Nobel Peace Prize winner for her work in India, is a modern example of one who protects her charges from a cruel death.

In some societies, those with specific handicaps were given distinct roles. Blind children were sometimes trained as historians, who committed to memory the history of the tribe or society. Blind people in other societies were taught to be masseurs. Court buffoons were often retarded people who provided entertainment to those around them, taking the brunt of the jokes of those who enjoyed making sport of them. Even in our present society, specific trades have been thought suitable for certain types of handicapped individuals: printing and cosmetology for the deaf; computer operations for the blind; switchboard or answering services for those crippled in the lower extremities; janitorial services for the retarded, and so forth.

Training persons with particular types of handicapping conditions in a variety of vocational skills has resulted because of past experiences with such individuals. They have been found able to learn if taught, thus justifying time, money, and effort spent in this area.

At one point in the development of care for the handicapped, it was decided to establish large hospital and training centers where both the physical and training needs of the individuals could be provided. These institutions were usually built away from population areas so that more normal people would be protected from the "inmates" and so those who were incarcerated within the walls would be sheltered from the cruel, outside world. The names of these institutions reflected their purposes—Home and Hospital, Hospital and Training School, Training Institute, and so on.

Another factor that contributed to the placement of retarded persons in isolated settings was the reaction to the ex post facto study of the Jukes and the Kalikaks. In response to the question of whether environment or heredity is more important in establishing one's functional abilities, a follow-up investigation was made of a Revolutionary War soldier who had impregnated a retarded barmaid while serving in the army and who later returned home to marry a girl of normal intelligence. The study examined the two sides of the family that had been sired by the one soldier.

As you read the results, you are amazed at the descriptions of the very successful types of persons that resulted from the legitimate side of the family and the slovenly, ill-cared for offspring that resulted from the illegitimate one. Heredity was seen as the only variable that made a difference between the two groups. The environment in which the members were raised was not considered important. These findings had a great impact on society. Many professionals and politicians panicked and felt that the only way to save the world from hereditary defects was to isolate all of those who were presently defective, to keep them from procreating, and to remove any who happened to be born into the community into some type of segregated setting. Sterilization was felt to be particularly necessary for any defectives who might have contacts with the more normal community.

The more able "defectives" *did* have contact with the community. The large, isolated institutional settings were designed to be as self-supporting as possible for economic reasons. Those who were minimally handicapped were taught the skills necessary to keep the institution clean and running. Farming and maintenance skills were often taught to the men. The women learned to cook, clean, sew, and care for the younger or more severely handicapped persons. In time, both men and women were allowed into the community to work for wages. They became "day help" and returned to the institution after their working hours. These capable people were later the first to be deinstitutionalized, and many became working, productive citizens in their communities. Deinstitutionalization came about after the recognition of the fact that many handicapped people had had their civil rights violated by being committed to isolated, often barren facilities, and it resulted in a change of attitude on the part of the general population.

Several factors led to this change in attitude with which institutionalized populations and members of classes and schools for exceptional children were regarded. During the 1960s, there was a great interest in the civil rights of all citizens. At the same time that the rights of individuals were being promoted, parents of exceptional children were demanding that their children be provided educational services within the local school districts. The benefit of institutionalizing very young handicapped children began to be questioned, and parents who were convinced that the home and community setting was a much better environment than an institution demanded local services for their children.

Educators were also looking at their successes and failures with the higher-functioning retarded. Their questioning of the value of special classes and of whether special education was justifiable for the minimally retarded led to a great deal of professional discussion which resulted in a series of efficacy studies that looked into the educational justification and effects of special classes.

In the early 1970s, the results of several court cases also entered into the discussion and helped steer the direction of special education toward mainstreaming many more children. In Pennsylvania, the parents of retarded children who had been excluded from educational settings brought suit against the Commonwealth. The court decree that resulted stated that all children, no matter how retarded, were entitled to a free public education. As part of the decree, children were to be placed in the least restrictive environment in which they could function, the most desirable and least restrictive placement being the regular classroom with their normal peers. Help from an itinerant teacher who would aid the student and teacher so that the child could continue to function was the second most desirable situation listed. A resource room, where the children could spend part of the day, returning to the regular classroom for the rest, was the third least restrictive setting listed. Self-contained classes, which were the primary service delivery system then used with even minimally handicapped children, were felt to be more restrictive than the resource rooms, but less than the residential schools that were also very prevalent during this period of time. Thus, by court action, children who were able were ordered to be returned to the regular classrooms for their education. A District of Columbia ruling broadened this decision to include all exceptional children.

A legal suit was also brought against the State of Alabama to provide treatment to those who had been institutionalized for emotional problems.

The decision in that case was that individuals could not be institutionalized without treatment being given, a common practice at that time. A court case in New York allowed parents the opportunity to examine their children's school records and led to much of our current confidentiality and record-keeping practices. A case in California mandated that tests given to children for purposes of educational placement must be given in the children's native tongue and should not be culturally biased against them. All of these cases, brought about because of the denial of the rights of individuals, helped pave the way to our present manner of dealing with handicapped children.

A series of laws passed by the United States Congress finally gave to all children throughout the country the rights that had been given to a few in individual states by court cases and state laws. These laws culminated in P.L. 94–142, which was signed by President Ford in November 1975 and put into effect in September 1977. This law, in essence, mandated education for all exceptional children in all the 50 states in the least restrictive educational placement in which the children are able to function. It encompassed much of the District of Columbia and Pennsylvania Right to Education decisions in this area. It legislated appropriate psychological testing of the children similar to the California court case, guaranteed confidentiality of records as the New York case had done, ensured protection of the rights of the children and their parents, and required a written plan for ancillary services needed by the children because of their handicapping conditions, as well as a written educational plan for each individual child. The time was right to pass such a law, and the overwhelming support in the Congress for its passage was almost unprecedented. The law is enforced by withdrawing federal funds from any state that fails to comply with the law.

As you can see, this legislation did not happen overnight. Those who worked toward this goal were rewarded only after long efforts. However, some classroom teachers who are unfamiliar with the long series of undertakings that led to this law have felt that the "sudden" decision to place handicapped children in regular classrooms, or mainstreaming, was mandated by local administrators. Many have fought the decision without knowing the intent of the law. (It is interesting to note that the word "mainstreaming" is not used in the law. However, the word has been attached to the placement of those handicapped children for whom regular classrooms appear to be the least restrictive settings.)

The confusion which has surrounded the meaning of mainstreaming was so great that in 1975 the Council for Exceptional Children, a professional organization of over 60,000 professionals working with exceptional children, published a list of themes inherent in the concept of mainstreaming. Their definition stated that mainstreaming is:

- providing each child with the most appropriate education in the least restrictive environment.

- looking at the educational needs of special children rather than at their clinical or diagnostic labels.
- seeking and creating alternatives to help general educators serve minimally handicapped children in the regular classroom.
- uniting the skills of general and special education for the educational benefit of the children.

Regular educators were not the only ones concerned about the concept of mainstreaming. Thinking that mainstreaming might dissolve the service delivery systems that had evolved for special children over a long period of time, special educators were anxious. Some worried about the quality of education that regular teachers would provide their children. Some knew their children were not ready for the regular classroom and would fail if placed there. Experience had shown some special educators that administrators seized mainstreaming as an opportunity for putting children into regular classes without support services. Some feared that school authorities would use mainstreaming as a way to cut their budgets for special education. Others were concerned about the emotional reaction of children placed within the regular settings, and still others were concerned that there would be no need for special educators and that they would be out of jobs.

Regular educators were worried about many of the same things but in a different way. Could they provide the services that special children need? Could they react emotionally to having exceptional persons in their classes? How would they deal with the regular children in their classes as to attitudes, questions, time? Because of questions such as these the Council for Exceptional Children also published a list of things that mainstreaming is *not*. It is not:

- the closing of all special classes for a wholesale return of all exceptional children to regular classes.
- placing the special children in regular classrooms without the support services they need.
- ignoring the needs of some children that cannot be met in the regular educational program.
- less costly than self-contained special educational classrooms.

Those who wrote the rules and regulations for implementing P.L. 94–142 were also aware of the concerns of all teachers. Written into the implementation was the idea of training regular as well as special educators for their new roles This book is designed to help prepare you to handle the children with special needs that are placed in your class.

CHAPTER 2
WHAT'S IT LIKE TO BE HANDICAPPED?

It is one thing to say that we will do a good job with the children who have been placed in our care and whose education is our responsibility, and another thing to do it. We were once children ourselves, and many of us can remember the hard times we had with many subjects as we attempted to learn them. Some of us can remember the flash cards that taught us our number combinations, some can remember the multiplication tables that caused us problems until we had them carefully memorized, and others can remember the little techniques that we taught ourselves to remember if *i* comes before *e*. Thus, we have some kindred feelings with the young children we teach and often pass on to them the little techniques we found useful.

If we have never been handicapped, however, it is very difficult to imagine the particular problems that handicapped children have in society. We in school can often make them very unhappy just because we place demands upon them that they are unable to meet. We can also make them just as unhappy by not having adequate expectations of them.

To make us a little more empathetic, let's suppose for a short time that we are handicapped. Only as we notice the feelings we have as we go through various experiences can we even imagine what our handicapped youngsters encounter.

LEARNING DISABILITIES

As we go through this book, we find that we are able to read the pages because we have learned to read, can remember the sounds and configurations of the words, and can put the words in the right order. However, some children have problems with these skills and cannot read the words as we do—the groups of letters do not make sense. These children may have perceptual problems and be unable to perceive the letters and words as we do. The letters on a page may run together, be reversed or upside down, or

7

they may be grouped into completely different words that the children are unable to decipher. See how you perform when reading the following passage presented to you as if you had some of the problems that children with particular types of learning disabilities have.

Cnilpreh mitn barticnlar broplews way rivir slillirs aup way hot de aple to make ont mnat tney say. Tneywa ysee sow ellillirs fo rotners, tne yway pron dtneeliloirs so tna t tne ybo hot forwmorbs tnat wake sehseto tne m. If yonstnby tnese wo rbslo hg ehongn yon snonlb de adle to fipnre ont mnat tney ar esayihp decanse yon nave nab certai nexderiehces tnat allomx yon to sndstitnte sow elillirs for otners ahb tneh to wake sehse ont of tnem. Tne cnilb mitn learhihp broplews nas hot nab tne sawe tybes of exderieuhces tnat yon have nap anp so cahhot snpstitnte ihtne sawewauuer . . . ne nas hever learhep tnem ah yotner may.

This may give you greater insight into why some children are so long in responding when you ask them to read. They have to figure the key to the funny looking squiggles found on the page.

HEARING HANDICAPS

Other children may have auditory problems that interfere with their learning. These auditory problems may be perceptual in nature or they may be the result of an acuity loss when there is something in the structure of the hearing mechanism that interferes with the children hearing accurately. In either case, the difficulty may be similar to the whispering game we played as children. The first in line whispered to the second, and the message was passed down the row until spoken aloud by the last person. The communication somehow always became garbled, and the message as finally spoken often had nothing in common with the original message sent. And so it may happen with children with auditory learning problems; the message that is received may have an entirely different meaning from the one that was sent. If you haven't played this game for awhile, the next time you are with a group of people, get them to play it with you. You make the first statement and also receive it from the last person to hear it. As you make the original statement, do it as if it were extremely important to get your message across accurately and without any error. When you receive the final message, imagine how you would feel if your credibility depended upon the accuracy of your reception of the original message.

The lack of hearing or auditory acuity is a very easy handicap to simulate. Try listening to the nightly newscast without the volume turned up on your television. Or place the volume a little below what is comfortable to really make out what is being said. By constantly straining to hear what is being said, we become irritated, or tired, or we react in some other way. We soon can begin to empathize with those who have a reduction in the amount that they can hear of the world around them.

Reducing the volume on the television is not really like being deaf, however. True deafness cannot be conveyed so simply, for we who are not deaf have had the advantage of our hearing to learn the language that we use each day of our lives. Children who are deafened before they learn to speak do not have that advantage.

Our language is such a difficult thing with all of its meanings that those who cannot hear it spoken are never able to gain the proficiency in its use that they would have if they did not have a problem with hearing. Hearing impairment has a decided influence on every subject that is taught in an academic setting. Missing speech is only one part of the problem; learning language also becomes a tremendous task.

ORTHOPEDIC IMPAIRMENTS

Another type of problem presents itself when children who have difficulty managing their muscles are asked to perform tasks that require more control than they have. If you've ever taken piano lessons you cannot help but be impressed with a professional's skill when playing a composition. You don't chastise yourself, however, because you cannot play with the same expertise. Sometimes, however, we expect all the children in our classroom to perform with the same degree of skill. We give timed tests and grade the children for the amount of work they can perform within a particular time period. Even intelligence tests are often timed, so that the child who is unable to react quickly because of insufficient muscle control is penalized because of a deficiency of skill in movement rather than a lack of mental ability. To simulate such a task, complete the activity presented in figure 2.1 in one minute. Pretend that the results will help determine your IQ and whether you will be placed in a regular classroom or in a special class for retarded children. To make the task more authentic, use your nondominant hand while you complete the activity.

In figure 2.1 you will find a set of boxes with letters from I to P. Below each letter is a corresponding symbol. As quickly as you can, fill in the appropriate symbol for each letter with an empty box beneath it. The first six boxes are samples and have already been completed. Get someone to time you, and do not exceed the one minute time limit.

Did you finish the test in one minute? If you didn't, how did it make you feel to know that your intelligence is to be based on your score? Or that you might be placed in a room for exceptional children for failing to achieve a particular score? This has been the way that some children have been labeled and placed in classrooms for exceptional children for a long period of time. Do you feel injustice? Rage? Concern for what we sometimes do to our children? The goal of these activities is to make you aware of the problems of the handicapped children you may be called on to teach, and to help you avoid contributing to the injustices done to them.

Figure 2.1.

I	J	K	L	M	N	O	P

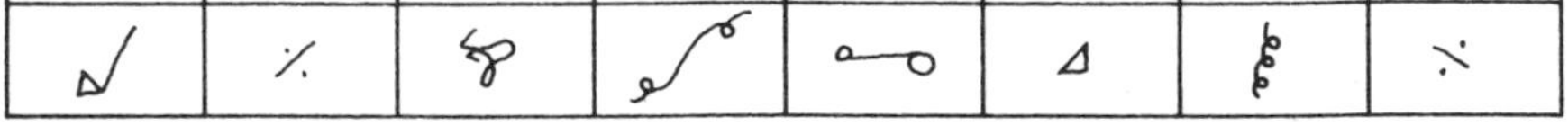

N	P	I	M	K	O	L	I

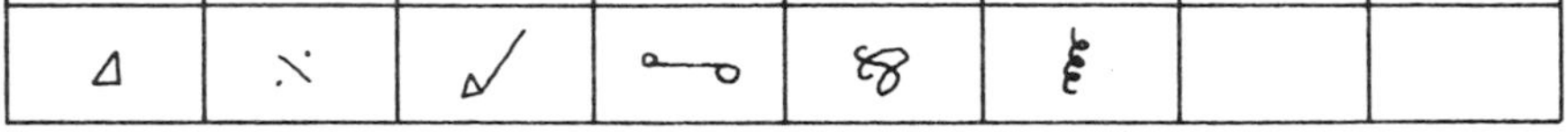

K	J	L	M	I	P	K	N

M	P	O	J	N	O	L	N

P	M	J	L	I	K	L	O

P	P	O	N	M	L	K	J

I	J	P	M	O	K	L	N

10

heard: "Those who can, do. Those who can't, teach." "Teachers make so little money anyone is foolish to go into the field." "That teacher couldn't make it in the world of business." "She doesn't know what she's talking about." "America is a land where one doesn't have to have an education and can still become a millionaire." "He may know a lot of stuff that's found in books, but he probably couldn't even rip off a car without getting caught."

Our job as teachers is to reach all of the children, no matter what their background and experiences. Only by being aware of the great diversity of those backgrounds, experiences, and handicaps can we hope to do a good job. Our mental attitudes toward the children have much to do with how we teach them. By becoming more aware of how they feel, function, and live with their handicaps we can become better able to help them. We've pretended to be handicapped. It is important to remember, however, that even if we really become handicapped today, we would not be like those we teach—we've had many years of education and experience as nonhandicapped persons. Somehow, we must find a way to give the same kind of experiences and education to those who come to us already handicapped.

CHAPTER 3
FEELINGS ABOUT THE HANDICAPPED

Helping children with problems is much like playing the role of a good detective. Clues are given that have to be considered in order to solve the problems. It is important, however, to know what type of clues we are looking for. What makes the children function as they do? We may never find the exact cause, but that should not keep us from trying to help specific children. We need some idea of exactly where to begin with each child. The only way to know this is to look at that child very carefully.

Any type of problem that children exhibit will need to be examined in three specific areas: the child, the task, and the setting. When children present a problem we need to know as much as we can about the children and what they bring to the task. We need to observe these children, to read their records, and to know as much about the type of handicapping conditions that they exhibit as possible. It is also important to know that the way we feel about the children will enter into how we view them and interpret their records. Our biases are often not even known to us, but they may make a big difference in the way we look at children.

A study was carried out in which teachers were told that certain children were potentially gifted and should make great progress while in each of these teacher's rooms. Other children in each room were not identified to make that type of progress. Unknown to the teachers, the children had been randomly assigned; those who were called potentially gifted were just regular children who had been labeled to see how the teachers would respond to preconceived notions. In effect, the children who had been labeled as potential achievers did achieve more than those who were not so labeled. The teachers' expectancies seemed to make the difference. Although researchers have not been able to replicate this particular study, other studies have been carried out that show that teachers often have preconceived ideas about how much children with special education labels can attain in their classes.

The attitude that you have regarding the mainstreamed children in your classroom will have much to do with the success or failure of those children while in your room. If you really believe that they will fail, rest assured that there will be failure! If you are determined to make a success, you'll find yourself going all out to ensure that success. This is the reason why we must determine if we have hidden biases.

Although we cannot be sure that we are ever completely free of preconceptions, we must examine ourselves periodically to determine how prevalent these biases are. One way we can do this is to make a list of things that come into our minds as representative of different types of handicapping conditions. Write the first ten things that come into your mind that describe someone who is *blind*. Then write the first ten things that come into mind when you think of someone who is *deaf*. Write ten thoughts to describe someone who is *mentally retarded*. Now do the same thing for someone who is *learning disabled* and *emotionally disturbed*.

Blind

1. _____

2. _____

3. _____

4. _____

5. _____

6. _____

7. _____

8. _____

9. _____

10. _____

Deaf

1. _____

2. _____

3. _____

4. _____

5. _____

6. _____

7. _____

8. _____

9. _____

10. _____

Mentally Retarded

1. _____

2. _____

3. _____

4. _____

5. _____

6. _____

7. _____

8. _____

9. _____

10. _____

Learning Disabled

1. _____

2. _____

3. _____

4. _____

5. _____

6. _____

7. _____

8. _____

9. _____

10. _____

Emotionally Disturbed

1. _____

2. _____

3. _____

4. _____

5. _____

6. _____

7. _____

8. _____

9. _____

10. _____

Now let us examine the responses that you have written. We need to look at them to see if they are inferential or if they are objective statements. Are they assumptions, or can they be considered as facts? If someone else looked at children who possessed these types of handicapping conditions, would they see the same things you have written? Are your statements measurable?

Let's think of some particular descriptions and try to determine which are assumptions and which are facts. If I say, "John is ten years old," that may be an assumption or it may be a fact. If I have John's birthdate in front of me, I may be able to determine that it is a fact. If I add, "He repeated first grade," that again can be verified by the records. If I also add, "He is one year older than the rest of the kids in the class," the natural inclination is to say that that is a fact. We know that John is ten and we know that he repeated a grade, so we assume that he is one year older than the other children in the class. However, John may have been a year younger when he started school. Or he may have been older than his peers when he began school. Or he may have repeated several classes and may be more than one year older than the rest of the children. We can only verify that he is a year older than the other children by knowing how old the other children are. It is this quick jumping to conclusions that can get us on the wrong track when we seek to examine children's problems. We have to be very careful when we know only some of the facts that we don't come up with the wrong conclusions.

We may also make assumptions that have nothing to do with handicapping conditions but are based on our previous experiences with particular children. If we have formerly taught a large, overweight, slow-moving retarded child, and our encounters with the retarded population have been limited to such children, we may assume that retarded children are typically large, overweight, and slow moving. We may draw the opposite conclusions if prior experience has been with small, wiry, hyperactive retarded children. It is important to know that, like all children, the retarded population comes in assorted sizes with varying dispositions, personalities, abilities, and ranges of intelligence.

Look again at your lists describing the various types of handicapping conditions. Are any of the words you have written value words, such as "good," "kind," "pretty," "dumb," "ugly"? Again, these types of words may be assumptions that you have made about the persons, whether these assumptions are positive or negative. If we're going to have biases, it is much more beneficial to the children involved to have positive biases rather than negative ones, for such biases will not prevent us from trying to accomplish things with the children. However, if we are so positive that we deny that the handicapped are not different from all the other children, we may not be prepared for the particular types of learning problems that they may exhibit. Thus we can do them an injustice by considering them the same as all children. On the other hand, if we consider handicapped children as so different that they can't learn, we may be creating a self-fulfilling prophecy.

It is important to examine the sources of our preconceptions of what these children are like. Are they based on fact? Have we known one deaf person and consequently base all our ideas about deafness on the functioning of that one person? Are some of our ideas based on prejudices that were embedded early? Have we heard a grandparent complain about the high taxes that may have resulted when extra millage was imposed for educating exceptional children and consequently become prejudiced against them? Have we read books in which exceptional children were labeled with such terms as "deaf and dumb," "stupid," "batty"? Have those types of words influenced the way we look at exceptionalities?

If we are going to handle a broad range of individuals within our classrooms, it is very important that we look at the children as unique people with strengths and weaknesses of their own, not as persons with personalities determined by a set of labels that have been conferred by some "all knowing" individual. Look at each of the descriptors you have given the children on your lists and see how many are words that contain prejudices or unfounded assumptions.

Each of us likes to be thought of as unique. We each have strengths and weaknesses. It is much more comfortable for all of us if we do not have to make sharp cut-offs when describing our own strengths and weaknesses. How are you at balancing your checkbook? Are you always in balance? How would you describe yourself if you compared your mathematical ability with that of a math professor? Are you on one side marked "bad" and the professor on the other? Or would you rather see yourself in the middle of a long continuum with the math professor much more advanced?

We all dislike categorical statements to which we are forced into a yes or no response. We very often will add, "yes, but only in certain conditions," or "no, not always." We may lack specific skills and if forced into a categorical yes-no response, we may have to reply that, "Yes, we are lacking in math skills," because we have trouble with a checking account. But that fact does not usually make us think less of our overall abilities, because we know there are other things that we can do, specific abilities that we have, that counterbalance those that we are lacking.

Can you carry a tune? Play a piano well? How would you compare your abilities with those of your favorite singer? Again, are you far apart on that continuum? If you played alongside a great pianist, would you be embarrassed by your lack of ability or skill? Should your lack of skill affect your life?

Unfortunately, some handicapped children have been labeled and forced into a very different life style because someone put them into categorical molds because they functioned at the low end of a continuum. Little effort may have been made to determine whether they were functioning there because someone was using inferential data rather than hard facts. Evidence in some court cases has shown that children were evaluated with instruments that tested reactions to experiences that the children had never been exposed to. The results of such testing often determined the place where these children would reside or limited the type of education they would be allowed. The future of these children was determined because the person who evaluated them inferred that they had had the types of experiences that the test demanded.

Let's talk about the backgrounds of the children in just one classroom who were able to begin their educations because of the provisions of P.L. 94–142 that allowed previously excluded children to attend school. One child, who was blind, had been excluded because she could not dress herself and would not chew solid food. Her mother, believing that blind children were not capable of such things, had always dressed her and allowed her to eat the soft food diet the child had long before become accustomed to. This same child had won first place in a piano contest! Although she had demonstrated competency in an area in which she had to memorize and produce in front of a large audience, she had not previously been allowed to be a part of an academic program.

Another child had been enrolled in school at age six. Because of an early illness, he had had vision and hearing problems the first five years of life. At age five, surgery allowed him to hear clearly for the first time. Another surgical procedure at age six, along with corrective lenses, allowed him to see normally for the first time. However, he had had an IQ test given him before the two surgeries that showed he was retarded. Because that old IQ record was in his file, the school refused to accept him, even though that test was no longer an indication of his functioning. A new IQ test had been added after intensive educational work had begun at age five that showed his current intellectual functioning to be within the normal range. However, the results of that test were not considered. The first test was given more credibility because it had been administered by the school psychologist and the other had been given by a psychologist in the private agency where the child had received the intensive work.

A third child was dismissed from school because of poor attendance. Her mother was extremely overprotective about her daughter's hearing loss. Afraid that any change in weather might bring on another attack of otitis media, she kept her daughter home at those times. The school spent no time trying to discuss the matter with the mother, but instead chose to dismiss the child, who had an above average IQ.

A fourth child had been through the extreme emotional trauma of seeing his father commit suicide. The child stopped talking at that point. Although he still continued to understand everything spoken to him and could carry out three- and four-stage directions, school personnel had refused admission to him because he had no means of communication other than a nod or shake of the head.

These children were not excluded from the regular classroom but from special education classrooms. Their cases were felt to be too involved for even special educators to handle. You can see why there were law suits over denial of the basic rights of similar children. Without a change in such laws, the children would have lived out their lives without an education. With it, all but one are now in regular classrooms because they have shown that they can learn and that the least restrictive placement for them is with their normal peers. One child is in a residential facility. The blind child has been placed in that environment so that she will be in an environment where her dressing and eating skills can be developed on a consistent basis. Perhaps after all these skills are developed, she too will join the mainstream.

To prevent these kinds of things from happening, we must make sure that the way we look at children is not determined by assumptions regarding specific types of handicapping conditions. We must make sure that we are observing children through very objective eyes, and that we are not perpetuating crimes that have been committed against children in the past.

In summary, then, we must begin to look at children—objectively, not inferentially—as functioning on a continuum, not as possessing sharply defined "can" or "can't" abilities.

If we look at children in this manner, we will also need to be much more careful in determining whether the behavior that we observe is indicative of a problem. Many of us, as children, learned that if we acted the least bit different from our accustomed behavior, our mother would sooner or later feel our foreheads and then come and put a thermometer into our mouths because "you feel like you might have a fever." Our mothers were doing exactly what we must do, verifying their observations. Unfortunately, we don't have thermometers that verify learning problems, but we can systematically observe and try to pinpoint the problems children exhibit.

Part 1
Bibliography

Bartel, N., and Guskin, S. A handicap as a social phenomenon. In W. Cruickshank (ed.), *Psychology of exceptional children and youth.* Englewood Cliffs, N. J.: Prentice-Hall, 1971, pp. 75–114.

Blatt, B. Public policy and the education of children with special needs. *Exceptional Children,* 38, 1972, 537–543.

Connor, F. Excellence in special education. *Exceptional Children,* 30, 1964, 206–209.

Dugdale, R. *The Jukes.* New York: G. P. Putnam's Sons, 1910.

Dunn, L. Special education for the mildly retarded: Is much of it justifiable? *Exceptional Children,* 35, 1968, 5–22.

Federal Register. P. L. 94–142, Part II. Tuesday, August 23, 1977.

Foster, G., and Keech, V. Teacher reactions to the label of educable mentally retarded. *Education and Training of the Mentally Retarded,* 12(4), 1977, 307–311.

Gallagher, J. The special education contract for mildly handicapped children. *Exceptional Children,* 38, 1972, 579–83.

Haring, N., Stern, G., and Cruickshank, W. *Attitudes of educators toward exceptional children.* Syracuse, N. Y.: Syracuse University Press, 1958.

Johnson, G. Special education for the mentally retarded—a paradox. *Exceptional Children,* 29, 1962, 62–69.

Johnson, G. O., and Capobianco, R. *Research project on severely retarded children.* Special Report to the New York State Interdepartmental Health Resources Board, Albany, N. Y. 1957.

Jones, R. Labels and stigma in special education. *Exceptional Children,* 38, 1972, 552–564.

Kirk, S. Research in education. In H. Stevens and R. Heber (eds.), *Mental retardation: A review of research*. Chicago: University of Chicago Press, 1964.

Lukens, K., and Panther, C. *Thursday's child has far to go*. Englewood Cliffs, N. J.: Prentice-Hall, 1969.

Murray, J., and Murray, E. *And say what he is: The life of a special child*. Cambridge, Mass.: MIT Press, 1975.

Nazarro, J. *How can tests be unfair? A workshop on non-discriminatory testing*. Reston, Va.: Council for Exceptional Children, 1975.

Rosenthal, R., and Jacobson, L. *Pygmalion in the classroom: Teacher expectation and pupil intellectual development*. New York: Holt, Rinehart and Winston, 1968.

Ward, M., Arkell, R., Dahl, H., and Wise, J. *Everybody counts! A workshop manual to increase awareness of handicapped people*. Reston, Va.: Council for Exceptional Children, 1979.

PART 2
UNDERSTANDING THE CHILDREN'S PROBLEMS

Exceptional children enrolled in regular classrooms will be those who have been thought will do well in that setting. They will be children who are more minimally handicapped than those who must be put into a more restrictive learning environment because of the severity of their problems. It is interesting to note that in some cases the degree of severity does not relate directly to whether the children will be able to be mainstreamed. This is particularly true in the case of acuity losses, in which children with a greater degree of acuity loss may be more able to function with their less handicapped peers than children who are more minimally handicapped.

You may also be teaching children who have greater problems than the children who have been identified as handicapped. Those children may be doing very well in the regular classroom and not be in need of special services. However, if you have such children with acuity losses, they should be referred for study whenever they are identified, for there are often procedures that can aid them.

Acuity losses are those sensory losses caused by a physical problem that results in a lessened acuteness in interpreting the environment. In other words, there is a physical reason why the children are unable to see or hear to their maximum ability. This distinction is used here to differentiate between children with acuity losses and those who are unable to see or hear because of perceptual or emotional problems. Children with perceptual or emotional problems have the physical organ of sensation intact, but the message that comes through that organ, although a true representation of what is seen or heard, is distorted by the person who perceives it. Thus, problems in interpreting the environment can be of a physical, perceptual, or emotional nature.

CHAPTER 4
HEARING ACUITY PROBLEMS

Deficiencies in hearing present particular problems in our society because it is such a verbal society. If we cannot hear what is going on, it is particularly difficult to learn language, which is so vital for success in school settings. We all learned language by listening and then imitating our parents. Our parents, in turn, reinforced our sounds, helped us increase our vocabularies, and gave meaning to the various words that we heard. Infants with hearing losses are unable to hear the sounds that they and others produce and, in time, cease the normal pattern of developing speech and language. With profoundly deaf children, every word that is learned must be taught. The speech that most of us pick up with little effort from our environment becomes a tremendous teaching task when children suffer from profound acuity loss. These children will have to be exposed to words and their meanings over and over, so that they can remember them.

Teachers who train those who will be teaching young deaf children point out that in teaching new words, most reading textbooks for first-grade children introduce a word and use it in context six times, after which the children are expected to remember that word the next time they encounter it in reading. Those who teach the retarded know that these children will be unable to remember the word with just six exposures, and they are advised to expose new words to the children six times the six times that their more normal peers are exposed. Teachers of the deaf know that these children will quickly forget a word that they rarely see and never hear, and so the exposure for learning such a word is more nearly six hundred times the six that hearing children need. Thus, the need for well planned repetition is great.

Children with less than a profound loss will receive information from the environment, but that information will be imperfect because of the hearing loss. Certain sounds will be missed, depending on the type and degree of loss. Voice inflection may be missed, as well as other factors that help us discern whether words are questions, exclamations, or noncommittal responses.

TYPES OF HEARING LOSS

In order to have a greater understanding of the types of problems that children with an auditory acuity loss might encounter, let's discuss the way in which losses are determined and the problems that might occur because of such losses. Basically, there are two types of hearing losses: conductive and sensori-neural or nerve. The conductive loss is caused by sound failing to get through the usual air pathways on its way to the inner ear. Figure 4.1 illustrates the normal pathway sound travels on its way to the brain for interpretation.

Sound goes from the environment into the outer ear canal and vibrates the tympanic membrane, or eardrum. This vibration sets in motion a small chain of bones in the middle ear. The last of the bones in the chain causes the membrane between the middle and inner ear to vibrate, and it in turn passes the sound vibrations into the inner ear. The fluid in the inner ear vibrates, and these sound vibrations are picked up by the little hair nerve cells inside the cochlea of the inner ear. The sounds are then transmitted from these hair nerve cells by means of the eighth nerve up to the brain for interpretation. This whole process is dependent upon the structure of the

Figure 4.1.

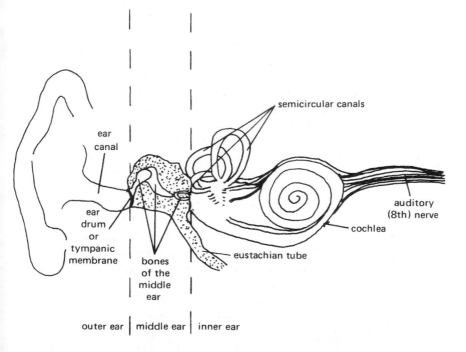

ear being intact, functional, and the nerve fibers all being able to transmit sound vibrations.

A *conductive hearing loss* results when the sound is not able to be transmitted by air across the outer and middle ear. It may be because the ear was malformed during prenatal development and the ear canal is too narrow. The chain of bones may be malformed. The eardrum may be missing or have an opening in it. Or the last bone of the chain that transmits the sound waves into the inner ear may be fixated and unable to pass the sound into the inner ear. The hearing loss that results because the sound is not transmitted across the outer or middle ear in the normal manner is called conductive loss because there is something wrong with the manner in which sound is conducted to the nerve. A conductive loss does not result in a total hearing loss because the sound waves can still be transmitted to some extent through the head bones and are able to reach the inner ear by passing through its surrounding bone.

To show you how the bones vibrate with sound, hum while you place your hand on top of your head. Now on your forehead. On your cheek bone. On the bridge of your nose. It is because sound can travel through the bone to the extent that the nerve cells can pick it up that there is never a total hearing loss when one part of the conductive mechanism fails to function.

A *nerve type or sensori-neural loss* is a very different type of loss. The conductive mechanism can be functioning perfectly well and the person with a sensori-neural loss will hear nothing if there is damage to the nerve that transmits the sound impulses to the brain. This means that the sound can go from the outer and middle ear into the inner ear, but something happens at this point to keep the sound from reaching the brain. It's much like talking into a telephone when the cord has been pulled from the wall. The message never gets through.

In the ear, some of the message may get through, however, depending on the degree of loss. Figure 4.2 shows us how. Suppose the coiled cochlea of the inner ear is unrolled. Inside we would find little hair cells that pick up impulses to transmit to the brain. For the purposes of this example, let's say that the longer cells represent the deep or low sounds. The shorter they become, the higher the sounds they transmit.

Suppose that some of the cells that are to pick up high and very high sounds are damaged and unable to transmit any sounds. That means the person would be able to hear sounds where the cells are not damaged but would not be able to hear those damaged high sounds. Or some of the hair cells that transmit one sound may be damaged but others may be intact. The sound may be transmitted but not so intensely as it normally would be. Thus the person with such a loss may hear but to a lesser degree than if all the hair

Figure 4.2.

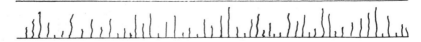

Figure 4.3.

cells were functioning normally. The number of hair cells actually functioning in the damaged ear might look as they do in figure 4.3.

INTEPRETING HEARING LOSS

In order to measure the amount of hearing loss that a particular person has, an audiometer, a machine that emits carefully calibrated sounds, is used. The sounds that a person reacts to are recorded on an *audiogram*. By looking at the audiogram a person who is trained in this area is able to determine not only the amount of sound that the person reacted to, but is also able to determine whether a loss is caused by a conductive or nerve type problem, or a combination of the two. The audiogram is illustrated in figure 4.4.

Numbers up and down the left side of the figure represent the decibels (dB) or loudness of the sounds being heard. The 0 represents the degree of loudness that is necessary for the average person to hear a sound. Since some people may have better than average hearing, the −10 is shown to allow for recording an above-average response to auditory cues.

The numbers on the left exemplify increasing sound at each level. The

Figure 4.4.

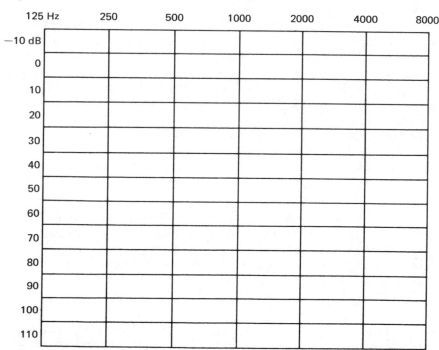

sound at 0 is very soft in comparison to the sound that is heard at 100. To illustrate the intensity of the varying sounds, 20 dB is the intensity of the average whisper. Normal conversational speech usually ranges from around 15 to 65 dBs. A shout is usually recorded at around 85 dBs. Some people are extremely sensitive to sound and they may experience pain around 100 dBs, while others may tolerate a higher intensity before they begin to notice pain.

The numbers across the top of the audiogram refer to the frequency (Hz) or pitch of the sounds generated. While sound capability may exist from 20 to 20,000 Hz, only those from 125 to 8,000 are measured in the typical audiogram. The 125 Hz is about the pitch of a man's voice while 8000 Hz is about one octave higher than the highest note on a piano. The intervals between 125 Hz and 8000 Hz represent about an octave between each marked frequency, with the pitch going higher as the numbers increase.

While the audiogram presents information across the wide range of sounds, those testing hearing will be particularly interested in the response the person being tested makes to sounds that fall within the speech range. Since it was already stated that normal conversational speech usually ranges from 15 to 65 dBs, it should also be noted that most speech sounds fall in the range from 500 to 2000 Hz. If we mark out the most critical area for assessing the hearing of a person as it relates to the spoken word, it would look like figure 4.5.

For example, the voiceless *th* (as pronounced in the worth tee*th*) has a high frequency, as does *f* and *s*. The child who has a frequency loss in the 2000–4000 level would miss those sounds when they are spoken. Since we learn to speak by imitating the sounds we hear, this child would probably leave out the *th*, *f*, and *s* sounds while learning to speak. A child with a high frequency loss might hear: "Mar ad a li am, i ee az ai az o" instead of "Mary had a little lamb, its fleece was white as snow."

Thus, the audiologist who is evaluating a person suspected of having a hearing loss will be interested not only in the amount of loss but also the frequency of the sound loss. Since conductive hearing losses do not block out all the hearing because some sound is conducted through the bone, conductive losses do not exceed 50 dB. This conduction through the bones can be demonstrated if we prolong an *m* sound and feel the top of the head, the cheeks, the throat, and the nose as we do so. By varying the volume of the hum we can feel the amount of the bone vibration increase and decrease.

Conductive losses can occur anywhere within the 0 to 50 dB range and are usually slightly dish shaped when plotted on the audiogram. Conductive hearing losses might look like those in figure 4.6. It can be seen that some of the speech sounds might be missing, but there are many others that will be heard, particularly if they are spoken loudly enough.

A nerve-type loss will appear very differently on the audiogram, for a nerve-type loss can occur at any intensity. The sounds that are heard by a person with a sensori-neural or nerve loss, when plotted on the audiogram,

Figure 4.5.

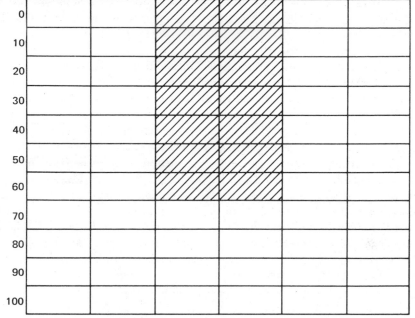

will usually have a steep slope (see figure 4.7). As can be seen in the lower audiogram, the only frequency in the critical speech area is at 500 Hz with a 60 dB loss. This person is probably unable to receive much speech through the auditory channel.

When a hearing loss is given as a single decibel loss ("the child has a 45 dB loss"), that single number is obtained by averaging the decibels plotted on the audiogram at the 500, 1000, and 2000 levels. Thus the resulting number is an average decibel loss and not a percentage and represents the average loss across the speech range. This allows us some idea of the amount of speech sounds the child is receiving.

Hearing losses are defined according to the average decibel loss at the 500, 1000, and 2000 levels. From 0 to 25 dB is within normal limits. Very often screening for hearing loss is conducted at 20 dB. From 25 to 40 dB represents a slight loss. Although it may have some implications for speech sounds, most children with this amount of loss are able to function fairly well in the regular classroom, particularly if the environment is kept quiet and the speech is kept at a fairly high level. Forty to 55 dB is felt to be a mild loss, while a 55 to 70 dB loss is more marked. It is this marked loss that makes the student miss many speech sounds. Remember that the majority of speech sounds require more hearing than this loss allows, and that the child will

Figure 4.6.

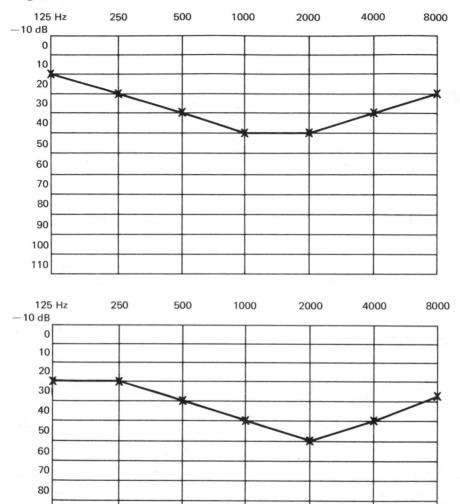

have to develop speech and language information in other than an inciden-
tal or untaught manner. Speech and language information will have to be
specifically taught. Children with 70 to 90 dB losses are said to have severe
hearing deficits, and those with less hearing than 90 dB are considered to be
profoundly deaf. The children with this type of loss lack enough acuity to
hear speech, and all speech and language must be painstakingly taught.

By defining hearing losses in this way, we may be misled into thinking
only in terms of the amount of decibel loss and the frequencies where they
occur. Some children with even a slight loss may need intensive help with

all speech and language activities, while others with a severe loss seem to pick them up very well. Although we can make a general statement that the greater the loss the greater will be the child's difficulty in learning vocabu-

Figure 4.7.

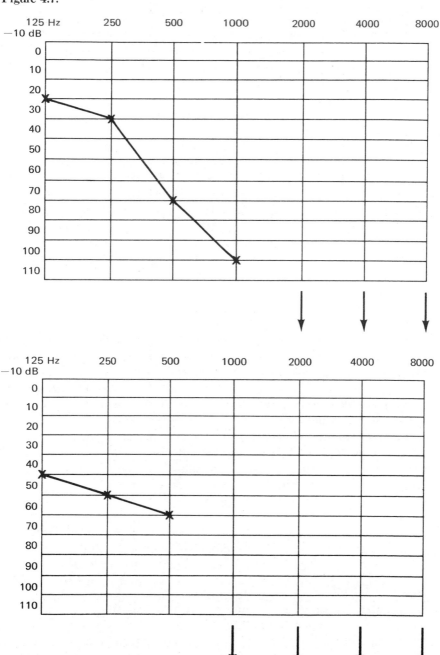

lary and language-based concepts, individual differences make frequent exceptions to the rule.

USE OF HEARING AIDS

The question of hearing aids often arises when discussing hearing losses. Exactly what a hearing aid can do is frequently misunderstood. A hearing aid might be able to aid those with a conductive loss, for it can amplify those sounds that are heard. Since there is a conductive reason as to why the sounds cannot be heard, the nerve part of the hearing mechanism is still intact and able to transmit the message to the brain. A hearing aid can often help the person who has such a loss by increasing the volume that is sent to the inner ear. Conductive losses also can often be aided by medical or surgical means. There are now eardrums, bones, and inner ear membranes that can be implanted surgically. Surgery is often helpful in cases in which there is some type of congenital malformation. For these reasons, children with conductive losses should be seen by a good otologist to determine whether there is some type of medical or surgical intervention that can help them develop more normal hearing, with or without a hearing aid.

A hearing aid will not provide lost hearing for children with nerve-type damage. Even though the sound might be amplified in the outer or middle ear, the damaged nerve will not be able to carry the information to the brain. Since nerve tissue does not regenerate to allow the child to develop hearing at some future date, the hearing loss from nerve damage is permanent and irreversible. However, children with nerve-type loss may still benefit from a hearing aid. If we again look at figure 4.7 and view the audiogram of a child with a nerve-type loss, we can see that the child does have some nerve intact; there is still usable sound getting through at the 125, 250, and 500 levels. Amplification with an aid may raise the amount of hearing in the speech area enough to help the child hear those sounds more clearly. The other lost sounds would still be missing, however, because the little nerve cells that pick up their vibrations in the cochlea are damaged.

One of the problems that accompanies the use of a hearing aid is that all sounds are increased, not just speech sounds. Since children may only be getting minimal benefit from an increase in the volume in the speech areas, they may have trouble sorting out the sound from the environment that is also amplified—chairs scraping, cars honking, ventilators rattling, water gurgling down a drain, and so forth. Many who are fitted with a hearing aid have a great deal of adjustment to make before they are able to put insignificant sounds into the background and significant sounds into the foreground so that they can be attended to. This is why it is vital that a well-qualified person test and fit the aid, and why it is extremely important to have good professional supervision when children are learning to use their aids.

If a child in your classroom has just received a hearing aid, you should work very closely with the hearing consultant to make sure that the child learns to use the aid well. Many aids remain in dresser drawers because their owners have never learned the advantages they can provide. Some children who have learned to use them well refuse to take them off, even while sleeping, because they know the extra environmental input that can come from them.

OTITIS MEDIA

Another factor that all of us who are teachers should be aware of is the incidence of *otitis media*, or inflammation of the middle ear. It is common among all children, but particularly among those who have hearing problems. Let's again look at the structure of the outer and middle ear, which is shown in figure 4.8.

The outer ear canal that leads to the eardrum and the middle ear are air-filled spaces. This allows the sound to travel to the eardrum without obstruction and the eardrum to vibrate freely. It also allows the ossicles, or tiny bones inside the middle ear, to vibrate freely and set the membrane in the oval window in motion.

In order for the eardrum to work freely, there must be an equal amount of air pressure on each side of it. The air is almost always automatically equalized because of the presence of the eustachian tube which leads from the middle ear to the throat. When pressure on the outside of the eardrum increases, we swallow, open our mouths, or chew to equalize the pressure in the middle ear. These actions open the eustachian tube, and the air rushes to the middle ear and the pressure on the inside of the eardrum becomes equal to the pressure on the outside of this membrane. Since the eustachian tube is not always open in adults, we may sometimes be aware of pressure and take specific measures to equalize it. We often yawn or swallow when

Figure 4.8.

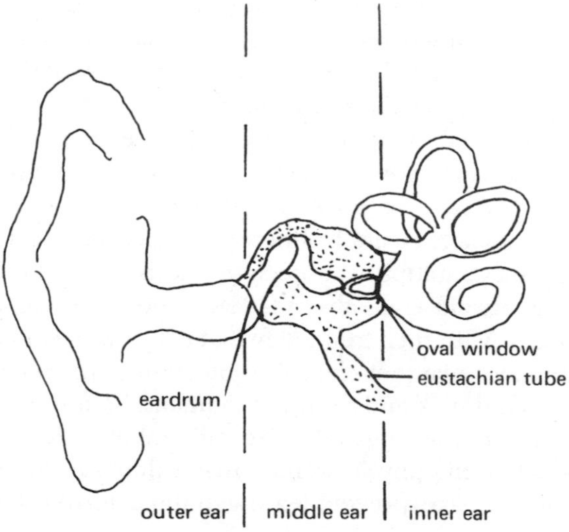

outer ear | middle ear | inner ear

moving up or down in a fast elevator. We may do the same in an airplane or while driving in hilly or mountainous country.

While the mechanism for equalizing pressure is a marvel, its very structure can also lead to otitis media. This is particularly apt to happen in infancy and early childhood because the eustachian tube is very short and always open in a young child. Although this allows for the rapid equalization of pressure on both sides of the eardrum, it also allows infection to travel to the middle ear. The middle ear is dark, moist, and an ideal location for the breeding of infection. If the child has a throat infection, the germs are able to travel up the open eustachian tube, locate in the middle ear, and multiply. In time, if nothing is done to interrupt the process, the germs multiply and produce a thickened type of mucous. This mucous can become dense enough to prevent the normal equalization of pressure in the middle ear. It may also become so thick that the tiny bones in the ossicular chain are unable to vibrate and a conductive type of hearing loss results. The infection may also result in such a blockage of the eustachian tube that all efforts to open it by yawning, chewing, and swallowing fail. If the pressure builds up enough, it may cause the eardrum to rupture, with the fluid coming out into the outer ear.

It is this tearing of the eardrum that can cause a hearing loss. Once the membrane heals, it leaves a scar that, if extensive enough, will prevent the eardrum from vibrating in its normal manner. To prevent this from happening, a physician may cut the eardrum to drain the fluid from the ear, thus preventing the eardrum from rupturing and causing a greater scar than is caused by a careful surgical incision.

Otitis media is the most common cause of conductive hearing loss. Children with a nerve-type loss are also prone to this type of infection and may have a conductive loss added to their nerve loss. There are two types of otitis media—acute and chronic. The acute type usually follows some type of cold or throat infection. The doctor may notice the infected ears while examining a child because of a sore throat, or the child may complain of pain in the ears. Prompt treatment with the right type of medication usually kills the germs causing the infection and the middle ear fluid clears. Permanent hearing acuity is usually unaffected if treatment is in time. It is important that the medication be taken exactly as prescribed. Patients often feel better immediately after taking a few doses and fail to take the medication for the specified number of days. The directions should be followed to insure that the infection is completely cleared. Otherwise, there may be a few cells that remain, and they may multiply and become the basis of another infection.

Chronic otitis media is another matter. It never seems to clear completely or it reoccurs with such frequency that it seems always to be present. The use of antibiotics may not clear the infection permanently, and there may be ruptured eardrums and frequent drainage from the ears. The fluid may have a particularly noxious odor. To prevent as much damage to the eardrums as possible, the physician may insert drainage tubes in the ears. These allow fluid drainage, prevent tearing of the eardrum, and allow some air to enter the middle ear. It is important to remember that children with tubes in their ears have an open middle ear, and anything that enters the ear canal can enter the middle ear. Such activities as swimming may be restricted or prohibited because of this.

Otitis media results in a conductive type of hearing loss while it is present. This is important for a teacher to know when she or he is dealing with such children. Otitis media may also account for some of the fluctuation in attending that some children exhibit in the classroom. On some days the fluid may keep children from responding to sounds, while on other days the children will react normally. Children with otitis media should be referred for medical care. Permanent hearing loss can result if the condition is allowed to advance without adequate medical attention.

INDICATORS FOR AUDITORY REFERRAL

Sometimes a teacher may have a student who has a hearing loss, whether temporary or permanent, and never have been aware of the student's condition. Following are some of the symptoms to look for that may be indicative of a hearing loss. Unfortunately, there are many losses that go undiscovered for periods of time because the children fail to manifest specific symptoms. If children exhibit any of the following signs, and particularly if they manifest several of them, these children should be referred for some type of screening for hearing problems. If the screening test is failed, an examination by a qualified physician is indicated.

Inattention, apparent denseness, and a tendency to fatigue or become confused may be indicators that children are straining to attend to what is being said around them, but are unable to comprehend all that is said. A tendency to turn the head so that one ear is closer to the source of sound may also indicate a loss. Children who omit sounds from speech should also be tested, as should any child in the class who is enrolled for speech therapy. Children who ignore, confuse, or don't comply with directions are also suspect, as are the children who don't understand what is heard. Children may also exhibit very loud speaking voices, for a hearing loss prevents effective monitoring of one's own voice. These are all things that the teacher should be alert to.

Hearing losses are often overlooked by parents in a home setting because the environment might be quiet enough, the parents' voices pitched in the frequency at which there is less loss, or the volume of the voices loud enough for the child to hear. Because conditions in a classroom are less likely to be "ideal," the teacher may be the first to notice a lack of or reduced response to sound. Any child who fails to respond appropriately to different sounds and voices should be referred to the appropriate personnel for screening tests. The very loud levels that are a part of today's music can cause hearing loss over a period of time. As a result, the increasing incidence of hearing loss should heighten the teacher's awareness of conditions that may signify such a loss.

CHAPTER 5
VISUAL ACUITY PROBLEMS

Children with visual problems have very different kinds of difficulties from children with hearing acuity losses. Many of us wear glasses, and so we think that we know what the life of a child with visual problems must be like. Our problems are very dissimilar, however. Children with visual losses are determined to have a loss for educational purposes only after they have received the best possible visual correction with glasses or contact lenses. In other words, their best correction is much like the problems that we have before we put our glasses on, if we have quite a degree of visual loss.

MEASURING VISUAL ACUITY

Visual losses, like auditory losses, are determined by comparing the visual acuity of the persons being tested to the visual acuity of the average person. Those who are legally qualified to do this measuring are called optometrists and ophthalmologists. We really should know the difference between these two types of people, because they have similar roles in some respects and very different roles in others. Both optometrists and ophthalmologists are trained to examine eyes and prescribe corrective lenses. The ophthalmologist, in addition, is trained as a physician and so is also able to treat medical conditions of the eye and do any surgery that is needed.

An optician is a third type of person who enters the picture, and he or she fills the prescription that the others write. In other words, opticians are the ones that grind the glasses or contact lens to the exact prescription needed. (Some optometrists hire their own opticians or contract with a specific lab to prepare glasses to their prescriptions. Thus, you may receive your glasses from the same optometrist who prescribed them.) Children who have a great deal of visual acuity loss and are using visual aids to help see to the maximum possible may be served by all three of these professionals at the same time, each one contributing a unique service to the children.

An eye doctor, either an ophthalmologist or optometrist, will evaluate children's vision in several ways—by assessing the distance vision, the near vision, the field vision, and their muscle control. Each of these measurements has particular importance for the child with a visual loss, for each plays a part in normal visual functioning. If any one of these factors is not functioning normally, it affects what the children learn from their environment.

Distance vision is normally measured by what the children see of an image that is 20 feet away. Just as the deaf are measured against those with normal hearing, the blind are compared with those who have normal vision, the norm in this case being what the average person sees at 20 feet. Thus, average people have 20/20 vision. This means that average people see at 20 feet what they should see at 20 feet. The figures begin to change, however, when people are not able to see as clearly as the average. Those with vision between 20/70 and 20/200 are said to be *partially seeing.* Those persons who see at 20/70 are not able to see what an average person sees at 70 feet but must get up to 20 feet of it to perceive it. The person who has 20/200 vision must be within 20 feet of what the average person sees at 200 feet to be able to see the same thing. We call these people with 20/200 vision or less *legally blind,* and the laws of this country allow those with this much visual acuity loss several free services to compensate for their acuity loss.

Even if children have 20/200 vision and are designated as legally blind, these children still have a great deal of vision, although it is far from what we wish it could be. Others with more serious visual problems may have far less than 20/200 vision, however. The amount of vision can decrease such that the children have little vision to distinguish details but might be able to distinguish objects they encounter. This does not mean that the children see them in the manner in which the average person sees them, but may see them in outline form enough to distinguish them from other objects that might be encountered. This is *object perception.* When we get up in the middle of the night and move around the house without the lights on, we move with object perception. We recognize objects and move among them even though we can't see them in detail.

Some children will have *color vision* and not much else. They can see the color of objects, but not enough else to determine what the object is. Even having this much vision can aid the children in recognizing particular objects, not from their shapes, but from their characteristic colors. One little fellow waited patiently for the bride to walk down the aisle and smiled recognition when a blur of white went past his aisle seat.

Still other children will possess only *light perception.* These children are only able to distinguish dark from light and nothing else. They are unable to distinguish colors or shapes. Even being able to determine darkness from light enables them to travel about more easily, however, for they can learn clues from the environment to help them avoid objects.

Just as very few children who are deaf have no residual hearing, very few blind children are *totally blind.* Those who are totally blind do not see the pitch blackness that we imagine, but have a total lack of vision or a grayness that becomes their world.

After the eye doctor has verified the amount of distance vision children have, vision is checked to determine how the children use their eyes for near vision tasks. Because most of us do not have near vision problems until we are middle aged, many eye examinations do not include a test of near vision. With children who have acuity losses, a near vision check is important to determine if the children are able to adjust their eye muscles so that they can focus on activities that are close to them. Distance and near vision require different processes. It is important to know if students are able to function at a near vision point since they are expected to do so much of it during each school day.

Just as distance vision is compared with average people who see an object at a distance of 20 feet, so also is near vision compared with average individuals. The normal figure is 14/14 inches. Such a reading indicates the distance from the eyes a child is able to focus on an object. Sometimes bifocals may be placed on children who have trouble with both near and distant vision. This allows children to make a greater degree of accommodation to see objects than would be possible without the bifocals.

It is not as important to know the prescription or the visual acuity of children as it is to know how much they are able to use the vision they have. The vision consultant should be able to help you in this matter. Observation will also aid you in helping children make the maximum use of their remaining vision.

Visual field is another factor that a good eye examination covers. If we hold our arms out at our sides and look straight ahead, we can still see our arms by using our peripheral vision. We can do the same if we hold our arms up and down vertically to our bodies. This use of field vision is very important to us in our daily activities. We walk down the street looking ahead, but are still aware of a branch hanging down just above us. Our peripheral vision gives us the clue. The same thing happens when we start to cross a street and a car comes into the peripheral vision at the side of us. We may duck or jump back without ever seeing anything definite. Our peripheral vision gives us warning and we heed it.

Those who lack a 180 degree field of vision are handicapped. If there is some amount of loss in the visual field, these people may have to turn their heads from side to side and/or up and down to take into account the vision that all of us get in one glance. This is particularly important in traffic, for crossing the street means a continual sweep with the head in all directions in order to be sure that no car is coming. By the time the last direction has been looked at, a car may have appeared in another area of the visual field and the viewer may miss it.

A condition called "tunnel vision" is a particular problem in the visual field. All of the peripheral vision may be missing and only central vision present. This means that vision is missing except for the very central part of the whole 180 degree visual field. Those who have such vision are limited to the same kind of vision that we have when we look through a cardboard paper towel roll. We have to move our heads constantly to try to see everything, and then in our minds we have to make a whole picture of the parts that we have seen. If the degree of vision is very narrow, the children may not even be able to see a completed word when reading it from the printed page, but must remember different letters and then put them together after finishing reading the last letter. Some children who must use magnifying aids to make the image large enough to be seen have this condition result. The size of each letter is so large, the entire word cannot be viewed at one time. Reading under such conditions becomes a very difficult and time consuming task. These children also have to have excellent memories to recall all of the letters and form them into a single word.

EYE MUSCLE PROBLEMS

A good eye exam will also cover an examination of how the muscles of the eye function. Our eyes are held in position by six sets of opposing muscles: horizontal, vertical, and oblique. If we move our eyes to the right, the muscles on the right side of the eyes have to tighten and the muscles on the left side have to relax enough for the eyes to move. The sets of muscles must be carefully attuned and move together so that a muscle does not move one eye more than the other.

It is when the muscles are not carefully attuned that we run into vision problems. One muscle may pull the right eye completely over to the right while the left does not allow that eye to move that much. This results in a malalignment of the eyes and in double vision when we look out of eyes that are in such alignment. An example of this is the vision we get when we cross our eyes and look at something. The crossed eyes result when the two sets of muscles do not hold the eyes right at midline. Cross your eyes and look at the printed words in front of you. Notice the blur? Any feeling of nausea? If you look at the words long enough there probably will be.

In order to keep a person who has such an eye muscle problem from becoming ill and to keep a double image from being sent to the brain, the brain learns to ignore one of the visual signals that comes in. In time, the repressed image fails to register on the brain at all. Just the one image is seen, giving that person a one-eyed view of an object.

Very young children who are just learning to use the muscles of their eyes to see are especially prone to muscle problems of the eyes. It is very important to have children screened for eye muscle problems by the time they are three years of age. Three years of age is a particularly important time because the repressed image will not have been repressed for that long a time period, and the ages between three and six are critical for teaching the eye muscles to function together.

An eye that is repressed is termed an *amblyopic* eye. The term *amblyopia ex anopsia,* or blindness from disuse, is the term that is applied to the condition that results from long-term repression of a double visual image. Just as there are degrees of blindness going from 20/200 to total blindness, this blindness from disuse can vary in amount. The problem occurs when the good eye of an amblyopic pair is damaged or the vision is lost from accident or injury. Those people who have two eyes always assume that there will be another eye to take over the visual task if one is damaged. An amblyopic eye will be unable to respond normally to the visual stimulus, however, and so the person who damages the good eye may end up at least legally blind in both eyes.

Amblyopia is a condition that responds to treatment if that treatment is undertaken before the child is six years of age. Although beneficial results have been achieved after that time, success is not assured. If caught early enough, the weak or repressed eye is stimulated as much as possible. This is usually done by patching the good eye and giving the weaker eye as much opportunity to develop the use of vision as is possible. Eye muscle exercises are usually undertaken after the patch is removed to try to get visual fusion between the two eyes. Surgery is sometimes undertaken if the muscle balance is so out of kilter that patching and exercises are of no avail. There may be a need to patch and exercise after the surgery to get the two eyes to function together. This is why it is extremely important to identify those children who are potentially amblyopic at a very young age—to allow time for all of the surgery and treatment that may be necessary before the child reaches the critical sixth year of age.

STRUCTURE OF THE EYE

The ways that the eyes are evaluated by the optometrist or ophthalmologist have been discussed. Now let's look at just how the eye is structured and why we see as we do. Figure 5.1 is a cross section of the eye. It is a view as if we were looking down from the top of the head and the eye had had the top cut from it.

Figure 5.1.

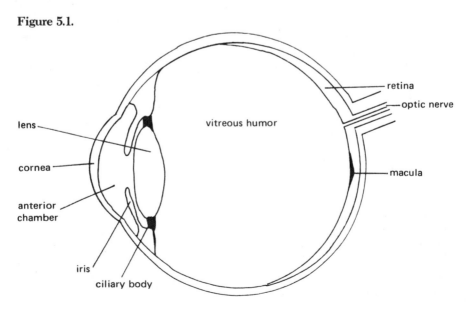

Light normally comes into the eye from different angles in the environment. The rays go through the cornea, aqueous (anterior) chamber, and then through the lens which helps the light rays traveling through the vitreous humor to focus on the retina. Since the most sensitive area of the retina is the macula, it is important that light rays coming in from the front of the eye be focused on this area or no color will be perceived.

If a child has a destroyed macular area of the retina, that person will not see color. The other areas of the retina help to perceive shades of gray and are particularly useful in helping us to perceive things in the dark. A child who has problems in this outer area of the retina will have "night blindness" and difficulty moving in dimly lit places and in darkness.

A child who has the macula damaged but the other areas intact may be able to compensate in some ways by paying particular attention to the information coming from the undamaged areas. If the areas of the retina outside the macula are intact, the child will still be able to see objects, but color will be missing. The child may be able to perceive some of the colors if only part of the macula is damaged.

Some children who are unable to perceive color may be able to distinguish the colors of objects by learning to associate the shades of gray they perceive with particular colors. Red is one gray while yellow is another. A friend explained how he never knew he was color blind until he underwent a complete physical exam for entrance into the army. Amazed that someone could get through his school years without really seeing different colors, we asked him to name the colors of different objects located around the room in which we were sitting. He accurately named each color, and so we turned on the television set to see if he could identify colors on it. The friend quickly named the colors, but we could not verify his choices—we were watching a black and white television set!

Visual acuity also demands that the eye, the end organ in the visual system, also have intact nerves leading the visual impulses from the eye to the brain for interpretation. The sixth nerve takes the impulses from the retina and carries them to the brain. Basically this is the way that we normally perceive. Just like the ear, the eye may be stimulated but a problem may prohibit the image from getting to the retina. Or the image may be carried through the eye and never reach the brain because the nerve is unable to carry the impulses.

ACUITY PROBLEMS

There are many conditions that affect the visual acuity of the eye. Some are diseases that result in reduced or lack of vision. There are acuity problems that are not diseases but result from structural differences within the eye. Two of these acuity problems are called hyperopia and myopia. They result when the length of the eye between the lens and the macula is too long or too short for the lens to focus the rays directly on this part of the retina. Figure 5.2 shows rays entering the normal eye. In the eye that has too

Figure 5.2.

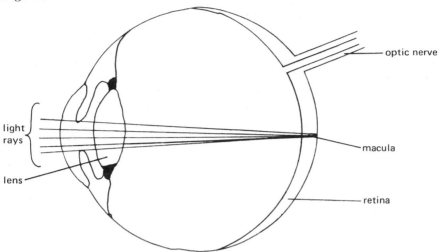

little space between the lens and the retina, the rays would focus as in figure 5.3.

This is either called a *hyperopic* eye or far-sightedness, because the person with hyperopia is able to see things that are far away better than those that are near. Because of the short distance between the lens and the retina, it is difficult for the lens to focus the rays on the macula area. Because close work requires the lens to focus even more than distance vision, the close work is more blurred while the distance vision, which requires less accommodation, may be relatively clear.

The *myopic* eye, on the other hand, is one that is too long between the lens and the retina for the light rays that come in through the lens to be focused on the macula. The point of focus of the most intense concentration of light rays comes before it reaches the retina, and the rays become dis-

Figure 5.3.

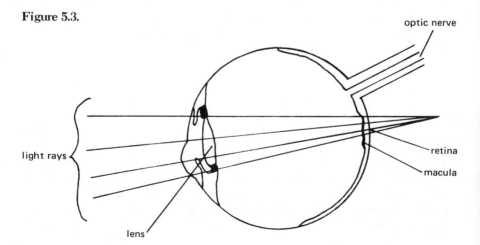

Figure 5.4.

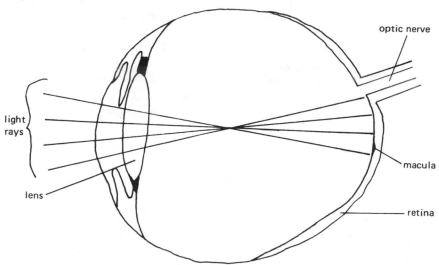

optic nerve

light
rays

macula

lens

retina

persed over a wider space on the retina when they finally hit it. Figure 5.4 depicts a myopic eye.

This is called *myopia,* or near-sightedness, because persons who have such a condition can use their eyes to see close work all right, but when they look up to see something at a distance, the vision is blurred. This is because the light rays coming in from a near point can be made to focus on the retina, but distant rays are widely dispersed over the retina and cannot be made to come into a sharp focus. People with myopia thus have a resulting blurred distant image that is transmitted to the brain. Myopia, or near-sightedness, is an inherited condition. Because of this, there are more and more people who are near-sighted. If you are myopic, chances are that your children will also be near-sighted, and that your parents are myopic.

Most infants are born with very small eyes. The eyes are hyperopic because the distance between the lens and the retina is very short, and the light rays cannot focus the image clearly on the retina. As children grow, the eyes grow too. Thus normal eyes continue to become less hyperopic each year during the preschool years. By the time children are about eight years of age, the distance between the lens and the retina has grown so that the eyes are no longer too short and the image is finally focused clearly on the retina. Up until this time children are not comfortable doing a lot of close work because of their hyperopia. Unfortunately, some teachers do not recognize the fact that many children in their classes are hyperopic and will demand a lot of close work completing the reading readiness materials that are prepared during kindergarten, first, or second grades. Fortunately, the size of the printed words in the materials used in these first few years of school is often very large, and children need not strain their eyes to see the letters. The wise teacher will require only short periods during which children have to use their eyes in intensive work.

The child who has large-sized eyes—meaning the distance from the lens to the retina—will be much less hyperopic during those first few years because the eye will be much longer and the lens will have to accommodate much less to focus the rays on the retina. Because the eyes are larger, these children do not have to wait until their eighth year or so before the rays come to a clear focus. Depending upon the size of the eyes, that period may come at age five or, if the eyes are even longer, it might come at age three. In this case, however, the eyes will continue to grow as the children grow in size, and the children grow right past the stage at which the rays are clearly focused on the retina and keep growing until the point of focus occurs before the retina. Thus, the condition of myopia results. While these children had normal vision at five years of age or so, by the time the normal eye has normal accommodation, the large eye has become a myopic one.

If you wear glasses or contacts and are myopic, when did you begin wearing glasses? If you have a fair amount of correction, chances are that you began wearing them by the time you were eight years of age. If you have less of a correction, you probably began wearing them during your growth spurt in the adolescent years. The rest of your body was growing and so were your eyes. They then went from the normal amount of length between the lens and the retina to too great a space for the image to be focused clearly, and you became myopic.

A third condition that presents acuity problems is that of *astigmatism*. This condition usually results because of some type of change in the curvature of the cornea or lens of the eye. It is much like an imperfection in a piece of glass and results in a change in refraction in the different meridians of the eye. We can be born with this or it might be acquired. It results in the light rays from images not focusing properly on the retina. Astigmatism can exist by itself or it can accompany both myopia and hyperopia.

INDICATORS FOR VISUAL REFERRAL

Because parents do not observe their children for great periods of time in the same types of activities that their teachers do, it is up to the teachers to attend to certain needs of the children, particularly during periods of rapid growth, and to be aware of any problems that the children might exhibit. Occasionally, children's appearances will give you a clue that there is something wrong. Although these clues may be a result of something other than a visual acuity loss, the fact that the conditions exist is enough reason to refer the children to the school nurse or physician for further tests. Sometimes children may be doing poorly in school, not because of a lack of academic ability, but because of a physical problem. If children have swollen eyelids and red-rimmed eyelids over a period of time, further study should be made. A crust around the base of the eye lashes, frequent sties, and red or watery eyes should also be looked into. Any time the eyes seem to cross, one eye or the other turns in or out, or the eyes appear to "jiggle" or be in constant motion, the children should be referred. If the pupils are noted to be of different sizes, that condition should also be studied.

Oftentimes children will have no outward appearance of anything wrong with the eyes. However, they may exhibit behavior that is not normal. Such behavior as rubbing the eyes frequently, blinking continuously, brushing the hands in front of the eyes, closing one eye or crossing the eyes when reading may indicate a problem. Tilting the head to one side while reading, holding the book abnormally close or far away, frequently changing the distance of the book while reading, inattention during reading class, stopping after reading very brief periods, losing the place while reading, and temper tantrums or irritability when asked to do close work are also indications that there may be a visual problem.

Sometimes children use their vision in ways that seem to indicate that they are having trouble making out the objects they are observing. Frowning when trying to view a distant object, thrusting the head forward to make out an object, holding the body in a tense manner when trying to make out something in the distance, and stumbling over objects may mean the children are having difficulty in seeing the things around them.

When children are reading in class or doing seatwork, there are other behaviors that may indicate a visual problem. Reversals during reading, guessing words from a part of the word, confusing letters such as a and o, e and c, n and m, f and t, and h and n are clues that can be used. A very short attention span while doing anything that involves copying, poor alignment when writing, losing the place on the page, deterioration in reading quality while reading aloud, and doing anything but what should be done when assigned reading may all be indications that the children are not seeing normally.

Referring these children for further study is necessary because, having never seen in any other way, these children are not aware that there is any other way to view objects. Therefore, they will certainly not refer themselves. If parents are not aware of the manner in which their children function while reading, neither will they refer them. Thus, it becomes the teacher's responsibility to note that a problem may exist.

It may also be the teacher's responsibility to follow up on the referral to see that the appointments are kept, glasses are ordered, and so on. Children sometimes fail to receive needed medical services because of some oversight, and the teacher should make sure that this doesn't occur. If the children are eligible for special services for the visually handicapped, the teacher may also need to act as their advocate to see that such services are provided. Most school systems have an eligibility criteria for services for the visually impaired with visual acuity of 20/70 or less in the better eye with the best possible correction. To be eligible for services available to the legally blind, children must have 20/200 vision or less, again with the best possible correction. Children who have a visual field of 20 degrees or less are also classified as legally blind. This means that the field of vision discussed previously is limited to less than 20 of the 180 degrees available to those with normal vision.

CHAPTER 6
MOTOR PROBLEMS

When integrating handicapped children into your classroom, you may find the handicapping conditions of certain students to be other than some type of acuity loss. One condition might be some type of motor problem. In years past, children were placed in special schools because they had motor problems, even though there was nothing different in the way in which they learned. Today, with our changing philosophy about handicapping conditions and the ability of children to function with their normal peers, children with varying types of handicapping conditions are more apt to be placed within the regular classes.

With the increase in accessibility that federal law has mandated for handicapped persons, there are many more motor handicapped people in the community than ever before. Motorized wheelchairs and the mandates for busses to be able to accommodate the physically handicapped will undoubtedly result in many more handicapped persons being seen in the future. Handicapped children were traditionally sent to one school where all of the therapists were centered and where the building was accessible to them. In the days when three-story school buildings were common, children were often denied an education if there were no elevator in the building. If there were not enough motor handicapped children in the community to warrant a special school, children were often left at home without a formal education, or with the services of the "homebound" teacher who visited the homes each week and left assignments for the days when no one called. This meant that children who were very bright but who lacked mobility were not provided an appropriate education. At the present time, however, children are placed in the regular classroom whenever they can benefit from an education with their nonhandicapped peers. Two of the more common handicapping motor conditions that will be found within the classes are spina bifida and cerebral palsy.

CEREBRAL PALSY

Cerebral palsy is usually a birth defect, but it may occur after some type of illness, injury, or accident when damage has occurred in the motor area of the brain. It is a condition that does not disappear with time—if a child is born with it, the child will live with it and eventually will die with it. However, many things have occurred during the recent past that allow cerebral palsy victims to have greater mobility and communication and self-care skills.

Since there is damage to the motor area of the brain, motor movements tend to be jerky or writhing. There are names for these types of cerebral palsied movements. *Spastic* is the name given stiff, jerky movements; *athetoid* the extraneous, uncontrolled, involuntary movements which are somewhat writhing in nature; and *ataxia* the condition in which balance is affected so that its victims move about as if they are drunk. These conditions affect the motor areas of the brain, but cerebral palsy is often accompanied by many other types of handicapping conditions, depending upon the areas of the brain that have been damaged. The amount and type of damage in the various areas of the brain determine the degree of motor involvement. Some cerebral palsy children may be merely clumsy or awkward. These are the children who weave when they walk down the hall, frequently raising one or the other arm to aid in balance. Their fine motor skills, such as handwriting, might be poor. Sports that require any degree of coordination are usually ones such children perform very poorly. Because of their lack of skill, they are the last to be chosen when their peers choose teams. Some of these children will never be diagnosed as cerebral palsied. The condition is so minimal that there is only rare referral for diagnosis. These children fall, bump into things, and remain awkward and clumsy throughout their lives.

The children who exhibit greater degrees of involvement of the motor areas of the brain are the children who are more apt to cause concern in the school setting. Some of the children will have all four limbs involved, while others will have only the arms, or the legs, or the arm and leg on one side of the body. Some children will have a fair amount of control over their extremities, while others will be unable to feed themselves, write with pencils, walk, or toilet themselves. Some may be unable to move at all.

It is important to know that there is not a correlation between the amount of brain damage in the motor area and the amount of intelligence that the children will exhibit. Intellectual involvement is a frequent accompanying condition in many of the children and retardation is common, but is not always present. In fact, some children are extremely bright.

Visual conditions such as strabismus and nystagmus are frequently present because, like all motor movements, they reflect damage in the motor area. Loss of vision in the visual field is sometimes present, as are seizures. The fine motor movements necessary for speech are very often affected, and speech problems are common, differing in degree from a slight slurring to a total inability to verbalize sounds. Because of the poor control over the oral muscles, drooling may result. Learning problems are frequently present. Thus, a child who has cerebral palsy may be one who is very minimally involved or one whose four limbs, speech, eyes, intellect, and medical well-being are all very seriously handicapped.

There does not have to be intellectual loss unless there is also damage to the intellectual areas of the cortex. This means that severely involved cerebral palsied children may have normal or better intelligence and yet be unable to care for themselves. In the past, these children were often sent to spend their whole lives within the confines of a residential facility for retarded persons, because those who were responsible for them were unable to see the normal intellect that dwelt within a crippled body and assumed that the mind was as damaged as the body.

Early intervention to prevent the many physical deformities that can occur if children are not adequately positioned, fed, dressed, and carried are now taught to parents as soon as the children are diagnosed. This means that many of the secondary handicapping conditions that previously occurred are no longer a necessary part of the children's problems. It means that even more children with normal intellectual potential will be found with their peers in the normal classroom setting.

If you have such children placed in your room, you may have children who are confined to a special wheelchair for the greater part of the day. The chair will need to be placed where the children are able to move in and out through the doorways easily. Someone may have to move the chairs if the children are unable to move their chairs independently. Some children may have to have some type of communication board that spells out what they wish to say, because speech muscles are sometimes affected to the extent that you may not be able to understand what is being said.

Communication devices vary. Some are designed so that children point to pictures on a board to let you know what they want; others require children to spell out letter by letter what they wish to communicate. More complicated mechanisms have electronic and computerized devices that spell out on paper or on a television screen the message the children wish to give.

The complexity and appropriateness of the devices the children use will be determined by the special education teacher and the speech, physical, and occupational therapists assigned to the children. These persons will be able to aid you and help you as you learn to adjust to the children's particular problems. The other children in the room may find it very interesting to note how each of the children is able to communicate and they may, if you treat it very unemotionally, be ready to make the extra effort that it takes to learn to communicate with the children and to take the time to become friends with them.

SPINA BIFIDA

Spina bifida presents another motor problem. Spina bifida is a birth defect caused because the two sides of the body's spinal column do not come together to form a complete circle around the spinal cord. Normally, the spinal column is formed by a series of small bones with a hole in the middle of each individual piece. This hole allows the spinal membrane and cord to be protected throughout the length of the spine and up to the brain. Spina bifida results in an opening on one side of one or more bones of the spinal column, and this opening allows the membrane alone (meningocele) or membrane and spinal cord (myelomeningocele) to bulge through the opening to the outside.

When a baby is born with this condition, the doctors will operate as soon after birth as possible to place the membrane and cord back within the bony protection of the spinal column. If they do not, the membrane may be punctured and the spinal fluid leak out, causing death. Failure to close the spinal column will also allow viral infections to enter the spinal fluid through the membrane, and the infection will then be circulated to the brain by means of the spinal fluid that flows inside the spinal membrane and around the brain. The presence of such infection can cause brain damage or death. Immediate surgery is recommended to prevent increasing damage and subsequent death of such children.

The immediate surgical procedures do much to sustain the children's lives. However, there are other complications of spina bifida that are not as easily remedied. Because the spinal nerves that are part of the spinal cord will have been injured as a result of their position outside and their subsequent surgical replacement within the spinal column, the functioning of the parts of the body that are innervated by those nerves will be limited or precluded altogether. Because the nerves that carry messages to those parts of the body are damaged, the children will not only be unable to move those parts, but unable to perceive messages that would normally be sent to those parts. For example, if the opening is high on the spinal column and the cord and membrane were both outside the body before surgery, the children will probably be paralyzed in all four limbs. An opening lower on the spinal column would probably mean that the children would have no sensation or voluntary movement in the legs. Since a high lesion may also affect the breathing mechanism, you are not apt to have such children in your regular classroom. However, children who have meningocele or myelomeningocele on the middle or lower back are often found within the integrated classroom. Such children will probably be on crutches and will have braces that extend from above the waist down to the feet to enable movement. The arms are not usually affected because of the lower location of the spinal opening, and so the children will be able to use their arms for independent movement. Such a low lesion also means that the children will be able to use their hands and arms in a normal manner and so much classwork will not be affected.

Certain children may have hydrocephalus (water brain) which often accompanies spina bifida. The drainage mechanism for the spinal fluid is affected, causing the amount of fluid in the brain to increase as new fluid is produced to nourish the brain and spinal nerves. In time, this build-up of fluid causes the bones of the head to spread and the size of the head to increase. This condition can be surgically treated by placing a shunt from the brain, under the skin in the neck, into one of the body cavities to drain off the excess fluid. Sometimes there may be brain damage when a blocked shunt allows fluid to build up which causes pressure on the brain. This may cause some type of intellectual, acuity, or perceptual damage. Such damage can be very minimal, however, and such children may be found in your room; or it may be extensive and the children may have to spend the rest of their lives in custodial care.

The major problems of the spina bifida children who are integrated into the mainstream of education will be mobility and toileting. Because the nerves are damaged, the children will be unable to perceive the need to toilet. Damage to the nerves affects the sphincter muscles controlling the bladder and anus, and so there is no voluntary control over such muscles. Because of these conditions, the children in your classroom may have had a surgical procedure to bypass the need for such sphincter control. The children will then have bags that adhere to an opening in the abdominal wall. These bags collect the steady trickle of urine and usually can be emptied after the children are out of school for the day. There are other devices that may be used so that the children need not be wet or embarrassed during school hours. The special educators, therapists, and school nurse can aid you with any questions you may have about a particular child's toileting needs.

Mobility needs are usually taken care of by crutches or by walkers, although occasionally children will be in wheelchairs. The children are taught in the preschool years to use their crutches and walkers appropriately. They are taught how to fall without hurting themselves and are given particular mobility training. You should keep in close communication with the specialists involved so that your expectations of the children's motor abilities are consistent with their potential.

Children with spina bifida have a tendency to be very verbal, and as a teacher you want to be very aware that their verbal ability may hide the fact that they do not have underlying concepts. Constantly checking to make sure that their verbal ability is based on solid basic concepts will prevent the meaningless verbosity of some older children who lack an adequate educational foundation.

MUSCULAR DYSTROPHY

Muscular dystrophy is a degenerative disease that differs greatly from the two we have already discussed because the symptoms of the disease do not appear for several years. This gives the children the opportunity to have normal preschool years during which their mobility is unaffected and they have full freedom of movement. Some children begin to show some symptoms during the later preschool years, while other children will show none until well into the elementary school classes.

Muscular dystrophy is a genetic disease that results in increasing muscle weakness that eventually causes the muscles to contract and thus cause crippling. Rare among girls, it is usually noticed in young boys when they are about school age. Their previously steady gaits become more awkward.

You may notice that they stumble, trip, or fall fairly frequently. One typical behavior that they exhibit is shown by the way they get up from a fall. The children use their arms to climb up themselves and straighten their bodies.

The calves of the legs are usually the first body part that is affected. There is a gradual replacement of the muscle with fat and fibrous tissue. The calves very often look large and fully developed and may even make the trouser legs so tight that the boys have difficulty putting them on. The looks are deceiving, however, for the calves are very soft to touch and without much tone. An increasing muscle weakness becomes noted in the pelvis, the trunk of the body, and eventually in the arms and legs. The increasing muscle weakness becomes so debilitating that the children may be confined to a wheelchair while they are still in elementary school.

At this stage, children with muscular dystrophy become particularly susceptible to infections. A simple cold can become critical because the children are not able to use their muscles to move the phlegm from their throats. Any type of respiratory infection becomes even more critical as the children lose more of their muscle strength and eventually end up confined to their beds. There is no known cure for this type of dystrophy, and the majority of children who exhibit symptoms during their preschool or early education years die before their teen years are over, often from a respiratory infection.

The problems the children present are often emotional as well as motor. The children have been normal and resent the loss when they become confined to a wheelchair. Many become quite angry. Others may have seen their brothers or uncles die as a result of the same disease and may be resigned to their fate.

Real problems exist after the children are confined to their beds because their lives become so limited. No longer is there a lot of stimulation and people involved with them. The lack of movement and worsening communication skills often make their few peers who do make the effort to visit them uncomfortable in their presence. This may lead to bitterness about what is happening to them. One way you can aid such children with dystrophy is to encourage the children within your room to make friends with them. After a child can no longer be a part of your room, frequent letters and notes to brighten his or her days can be used as good writing exercises for the other children to carry out.

There are other motor problems that may be observed within the regular classroom. Children with hemophilia, a coagulation problem which can result in uncontrolled and even spontaneous bleeding, may have damage to their joints which results in impaired or painful movement. Children with sickle cell anemia may be similarly affected. Other conditions can also result in various types of motor problems. If you notice children with impaired motor movements, a discussion with the school physician, nurse, or special educator may disclose some type of motor disability that calls for classroom modification.

CHAPTER 7
CHRONIC HEALTH PROBLEMS

Another type of problem that can result from damage to the brain is seizures. Seizures are very frightening to observe if they have never been seen before. High fevers or any type of head injury can bring them on, but they may also be congenital with some children seizuring immediately after birth.

The important thing to remember if a child seizures while in your classroom is to remain calm. The child who experiences the seizure will have no recollection of it, and so your behavior during the event will have much to do with the manner in which the children in your classroom are affected. An early experience can illustrate how very important it is that the teacher remain calm should such an event occur.

One of the girls in a sixth-grade classroom seizured just before the noon lunch break. The teacher became hysterical and went running into the fifth-grade classroom next door. The children in the sixth-grade classroom became upset, many cried, and general confusion reigned. It spread to the fifth-grade classroom as that teacher ran out of the room and into the sixth-grade class. The fifth-grade teacher reappeared a few minutes later to announce that the class was dismissed for lunch. Fifth graders tried to gain as much information as possible from their sixth-grade friends, and many tales of horror were told, often in direct conflict with each other.

The "fit" was the major topic of conversation as the children walked home. It was also the topic of conversation during lunch in many of the homes. In one, the question was raised as to what made "fits" and what they really were. A nonemotional response was given by the mother. A younger child, a first grader, responded that that was what her friend Mary Lynn had. The mother questioned whether the Mary Lynn referred to was the one that came by quite often to play. Assured that it was, the mother replied that she hadn't known that Mary Lynn had seizures. Asked how often they occurred, the first grader replied that they were often. In fact, so often that the teacher had placed a cot in the room so that the child could rest following the seizures. Asked why she had never mentioned this fact before, the first

54

grader replied that the first time that it happened, the teacher had told them that what was occurring was called a seizure and that Mary Lynn would not remember it when it was over. She told the children that Mary Lynn would probably feel really awful if the children made fun of her or if they told everyone about something that she couldn't help. How different the two children's attitudes toward seizures! One child could barely wait to get home to talk about the "fit," while the younger child seemed to have a rational acceptance of the problem.

It becomes the teacher's responsibility, then, for setting a tone of acceptance for the rest of the children. Discussing what is happening the first time that a seizure occurs and talking about things the children might do to help is vital. A calm voice and manner are necessary. Basically, a seizure can be described in terms of an electrical circuit. If too much is demanded of an electrical circuit, a fuse is blown. The same thing happens in the brain. Normally there is electrical energy within the brain. If too much of this electrical energy is released at one time, the result is a seizure.

There are many types of seizures. A petit mal ("little bad") is a seizure in which the child has only a momentary loss of consciousness. It is not long enough for the child to drop to the floor. The behavior observed may vary from child to child. It may be a momentary blank gaze, a blink of the eyes, a squint, or tic-like behavior. It is over in seconds. Such behavior may occur rarely, or it may occur hundreds of times a day. Grand mal ("big bad"), on the other hand, results in the child losing consciousness and falling to the floor. There may be a thrashing around, drooling, a blue color, and some children may urinate. The eyes may turn up, and all parts of the body may twitch. Children who have grand mals usually have some type of warning, or aura. They may see or smell something a short time before they seizure. This aura may give them time to get to a safe setting. Some children will drop to the floor when such a warning comes. Others may call out.

It is important that you know what type of warning the children may have and try to recognize the behavior that comes with such warnings. This will allow you and your other students time to move back the desks or move the affected children so that there is room for the thrashing of the hands and legs that may take place. This will prevent injury to the children that can be caused by the very strenuous movements that may result. Other than allowing the children complete freedom to thrash about and turning their heads so that saliva can run out of their mouths, there is little that you can do to help them during a seizure. It used to be that objects were placed between the teeth to prevent the children from biting their tongues. The bites that resulted during the attempts to place such objects, the broken teeth, and the bent spoons all attest to the problems that such placement entails. Although the children may suffer tongue bites, it is now felt safer to merely turn their heads to one side.

After children are finished with the active seizure, they will usually feel very groggy and want to sleep. Taking them to the nurse's room, placing them on a cot within your room, or placing them on a rug and covering them with a blanket in a quiet place are all means of dealing with this need for rest. The children will awaken later, remembering nothing of the attack, although some children will report sore muscles from all of the activity during the seizure.

Children, of course, are not learning while undergoing a seizure and while sleeping afterwards. Considerable time may be lost by children who seizure frequently. It is necessary that you later go over the material you covered while the children were seizuring, just as you would go over material that children miss while absent because of illness. For those who seizure often, you may appoint a particular "peer teacher" for the children to seek out and get information from following a seizure.

Most children with seizures can have their attacks brought under control by the carefully monitored use of medications. Children and parents need to be aware of the importance of taking the full prescribed dosage of medicine at the times it is prescribed. Taking the drugs on an intermittent basis, or running out and waiting to refill a prescription, may result in a seizure.

After the initial stage when different medications are prescribed at different levels, children usually have little trouble as long as the doctor monitors for growth and change. Most children will have seizure-free years. A few will have seizures once or twice a year, and those may occur out of the school environment. Other children may have partially or poorly controlled seizures. These will be the children who may have seizures within the room and for whom you should prepare yourself.

Various information is available from the National Epilepsy Foundation. Many cities have offices within their limits. Contacting either the national or local offices can bring free literature on just about any question you may have regarding epilepsy. This group even has pamphlets available for classroom teachers, and you may want to order these packets for any of the other teachers who will come into contact with the children who have frequent seizures.

The school nurse and the children's parents should be notified of any seizures that the children experience. Medical help should be sought if the seizures go on for as long as 15 minutes. Since most seizures are over in a matter of a few minutes—although it may seem longer—any prolonged seizure may mean that the child is experiencing difficulty and should be under medical care immediately. Sometimes spina bifida children will seizure when the shunt to relieve hydrocephaly has been blocked. It becomes very important in this case to get the children under immediate medical care to relieve the pressure that has built up. Otherwise the pressure may damage the visual or auditory nerves if not attended to within a very short time.

The children's doctors may ask you to report on their behaviors after there has been a change in medication. Keeping careful data on the children's behaviors will aid the physicians in judging the adequacy of their prescriptions. One teacher-pediatrician team was able to reduce the number of seizures by a third by careful documentation and cooperation. Data were collected on behaviors antecedent and subsequent to the seizures. This demonstrated that some of the seizures were self-induced to avoid school-work. Most seizure behavior is medical in origin. However, meticulous attention to data collection can aid both you and the pediatrician in noting changes in behaviors that may indicate a need for any modifications in treatment, behavioral or medical. Again, it is important to remember that your attitude will do much to make the children with uncontrolled seizures comfortable with the fact that they have seizures and will do much to help the children in the room to accept the seizuring behavior.

There are many other types of behavior you may observe in children that are the result of chronic medical conditions. Conditions such as severe allergic reactions and asthma may well be found among the children assigned to your classroom.

CYSTIC FIBROSIS

Cystic fibrosis is a chronic, noncontagious lung disease that is hereditary and caused by an inborn error of metabolism which results in a lack of the enzyme essential for normal functioning of the body. The production of mucous, saliva, and sweat are affected by the metabolic error. The mucous becomes sticky and gluelike in consistency, clogging air passages and the pancreas. This means that respiration is affected, as well as digestion. Children who are afflicted have a persistent cough from the clogged lungs. It is necessary to use frequent postural drainage to clear their air passages because they are not able to do it normally by coughing. Children often must be kept in a mist to enable easier breathing. Between the need for mist and frequent postural drainage, the children may miss school frequently.

It is necessary that children with cystic fibrosis avoid any viral infections that children in the classroom might have because these viral infections can cause severe and even fatal illness. Isolation from viruses and preventive doses of antibiotics on a regular basis are methods used to protect the children. The digestive tract is affected and the children need a special diet to meet their needs, for important secretions are prevented from reaching the intestines. The abnormality in this area results in undernourished-looking children who eat twice as much as their unaffected peers.

The children are usually diagnosed by the amount of salt in their sweat. Children who have difficulty breathing, suffer respiratory problems, and have huge appetites are good candidates for such testing. The great amount of salt in the sweat creates another health hazard for the children—there is danger of dehydration in hot weather. Children may be kept home from school if the weather is unusually warm and the school classroom is not air conditioned.

Not too long ago, children with cystic fibrosis died before their second birthdays. With the techniques mentioned above, this is no longer true, although there are still infants and toddlers that fail to survive past toddler age. Most children, however, are now able to survive through their school years.

DIABETES

Juvenile diabetes is a condition that is increasing in incidence. Another genetic disease, an offspring of two parents with recessive genes can demonstrate juvenile diabetes, a more severe form than the adult form with which most of us are familiar. The earlier the onset of juvenile diabetes, the more severe its implications in this most common of inborn metabolic errors. Diabetes is a leading cause of blindness and usually results about 20 years from onset. Diabetes is caused because there is an abnormality in the way that the body reacts to sugars and starches, allowing glucose to accumulate in the blood because it cannot be used normally by the cells. This glucose spills over into the urine, and it is by this means that it is diagnosed and monitored.

Once the disease is determined, the children must adhere to a strict diet and daily injections of insulin for the rest of their lives. Since insulin only controls symptoms and does not effect a cure, children have to learn that they must carefully balance what they eat with the amount of exercise they do and the amount of insulin they receive. Active children usually resent this adherence to such careful routines and restrictions, but any straying from them usually results in symptoms that are more unpleasant for them, and they learn that one is better than the other.

The children learn to recognize the symptoms of an insulin reaction and you should too. It happens quickly and immediate help is needed. If the child can swallow, sugar, candy, or fruit juice should be given. If the child is not conscious enough to administer these things by mouth, a quick trip to the hospital is indicated. Time is very important and caution should be shown. If in doubt, get the child immediate care. You should watch for the mild symptoms of faintness, trembling, shakiness, hunger, excessive perspiration, nausea, headache, or fatigue. In time these will get worse if ignored, and children begin to see double, stagger, become extremely irritable, experience difficulty in talking, and fall into unconsciousness, perhaps convulsing. Insulin reaction is caused because there is an inappropriate amount of insulin in the body.

A diabetic coma is a different thing. It comes on much more slowly than insulin reaction. Where the other can occur in minutes, coma can build up over a longer period, even days. Excessive thirst, a fruity odor to the breath, a loss of appetite, blurred vision, dry tongue, deep and labored breathing, cramps in the stomach or legs, flushing of the face, dry skin, a rapid pulse, drowsiness, and eventual unconsciousness occurs. Children should be under medical care immediately when you notice these symptoms.

One of the first things that teachers of diabetics usually notice is the irritability or temperament that the children exhibit when they are experiencing difficulty with their blood sugar levels. Discussion with the parents over particular symptoms they have noticed in the past can be helpful in knowing what to expect. It is important that the children not know that you are overly concerned about any of the medical conditions that they have, and that they be allowed to be as normal in their participation as possible.

OTHER CONDITIONS

Sickle cell anemia results from another error in metabolism. Children with sickle cell anemia trait will exhibit no symptoms of the disease. However, this condition is a chronic genetic disease that can result when two people with sickle cell trait have an offspring. Although there are increasing means of effectively dealing with this problem, children may have acute attacks when they will need hospitalization. Pain is acute. The disease, which is a result of an abnormality of the blood cell the shape of which gives the disease its name, can result in swollen and painful joints. Thus, there may be resulting motor problems. Recent advances are increasing the 20-year life spans previously predicted for such children.

Hemophilia, a disease that is rare in females, results from a lack of a blood clotting factor. Another genetic disease, it can result in internal bleeding that can cause death if undetected. Children with the condition bruise easily, with bleeding occurring under the skin. It is necessary to keep the children active without allowing them to inflict any injuries that can cause bleeding. Before the discovery of the concentrate of the blood clotting factor, the children spent long periods of time in the hospital receiving blood transfusions. Bleeding often seeped into the joints of the knees, elbows, and ankles, leaving painful joints that were difficult to heal. The severe crippling conditions that occurred because of this damage to the joints is not now as prevalent. However, it is still important that the children take no unnecessary risks that may start some type of internal bleeding or external injury.

Congenital heart defect is another condition that may be found in the classroom. These children were doomed to a short life prior to open heart surgical procedures, but now most of them are operated on very shortly after birth and will have greatly lengthened, if not normal, life spans. The children's health records will inform you as to whether there should be any limitations to their activities. Most of the children will be able to partake in the regular routine. Some records will note that the heart condition is "self-limiting." In a self-limiting condition, the children usually pace themselves in what they do without any reminders on your part. Over-exertion results in the children being uncomfortable and stopping to rest or slowing down. You can monitor the conditions somewhat by noting the color of the children's lips, the area around the mouth, and their nails, particularly at the base.

When the children have over-exerted and there is too little oxygen in the bloodstream, the coloring turns gray or blue. This is a time to step in and see that the children do something less strenuous. Unusual fatigue is another indicator for such children, and fatigue in a usually active child should be questioned.

Most of these chronic health conditions will not affect the children's learning, and so adjustments will not have to be made in the manner in which you present the material. It will be important, however, to have good communication with the parents, school nurse, and the children's medical specialists in order to be prepared for emergencies and to recognize the behaviors that may precede such emergencies. Prevention is always good when dealing with any type of atypical behavior, but it is particularly important when dealing with children whose lives may depend upon your quick actions. This should not frighten you any more than would learning coronary resuscitation because your husband or father has a heart condition, or taking first aid treatment so that you can deal with emergencies when your class is on a field trip. Chances are that the training will never be needed, but if it is, you will be prepared.

CHAPTER 8
SLOW LEARNERS AND INTERFERING BEHAVIORS

Children who learn at a different rate than the rest of the children in the classroom present particularly frustrating problems to the classroom teacher. It seems as if there are always a few children in the room who seem to learn at this different rate. At one time, teacher trainers spoke of the "hard core 20 percent," the few children that were unable to learn in the same manner and at the same rate as the rest of the children in the class. At that time, all children were taught from the same textbooks and were expected to learn at the same rate. There always seemed to be about 20 percent of the class who were unable to do it.

We now know that part of the reason 20 percent of the children were unable to make it was because the teachers failed to individualize for their needs. These were the children who later went into special education classes and are the same kinds of individuals who are currently being mainstreamed back into the regular classrooms, because special classes were less advantageous for them than the regular setting.

SLOW LEARNERS

Slow learners do not necessarily learn differently from other children. They do, however, learn at a different rate. Although the different rate of learning is the only thing that appears to be different from the other children in the room for some, others may show a different rate of learning along with disruptive behaviors we will discuss later in the chapter. For a teacher who is concerned about the amount of time that it takes to teach particular concepts and who is anxious to have all children complete the same amount of material during the year, the children who demonstrate these combinations of behavior can be particularly frustrating.

We will discuss only the behaviors relating to the process of slow learning here. The slow learner is the child who usually learns in the same manner as the other children but at a slower rate. The children may have a rate of learning as slow as one half of that of the other children. This may mean that it will take twice as long for them to learn specific tasks. It definitely means that the children must have their work broken down into greater detail before they are able to conceptualize it. These are the children, who, after you have presented a new concept to your class and then assign some work so that they can apply the new concept, are unable to do it. They may sit, completely bewildered by the activity, or they may attempt it and give up in disgust a few minutes later. These children are consistent in this reaction, no matter what you are introducing. They are slower in every subject, are in your "slow groups," are the last to finish their papers, and even the last to leave the room or to finish their lunches. They have often been labeled "dreamers," for they seem to be somewhere else when you are teaching.

Such children are usually attending as well as the other children in the class, however. They may be trying particularly hard to follow you, but their processing powers are unable to keep up with your presentations. They may not be able to attend for the whole period that you have set aside for a subject; they may have been lost since shortly after you started talking.

These children not only need to have the task broken down into greater detail than do the rest of the children, but such children need more time to complete their activities. If you are a teacher who demands that all children complete their work before they go out for recess or to the lunchroom, these are the children who are still in your room when the others come back from recess and the ones that you have to send to the lunchroom at the last minute for fear they will miss their lunches. No matter how you motivate them, they never seem to process faster and never seem to work faster. Your big goal in the past was to motivate them into more productive behavior.

Such children may be unable to understand abstractions. Illustrations frequently mean nothing to them. They may be able to learn facts very well but be unable to apply them. They laboriously master the multiplication tables but may have little understanding of how the tables are derived. Slow children may not be able to respond to teaching when it is presented in only one modality. They may need to see it to understand it. Silent reading may mean little, and they may need to hear words aloud to get the concept. Some may need to see, hear, and feel before an impression is made.

Many of the children are "good children" and so fail to give you cues that you have lost them. They sit quietly, not disturbing anyone, but not learning either. Those who have disruptive behaviors in addition to their slow rates of learning will let you know that they are lost, not by telling you directly, but by their disruptive behavior. Thus, such children are more able to be spotted by their behaviors because they let us know. The quiet children do not.

Some slow children may be extremely resistive to letting you as the teacher know that there are problems because of the attention that it brings to the fact that they don't know. Being slow in everything can be extremely debilitating to one's self image. Being very attentive to the looks on the children's faces as you introduce new topics is often the only cue that you will receive that the subject has not been grasped.

One way of dealing with these children is to allow more time in your initial presentations and in the amount of time you allow for them to complete activities. It will save time in the long run, for these children usually are not capable of more. Specific ways of presentation appropriate for them will be discussed in Part III, when we talk about analyzing the tasks to be taught.

Individual differences are frequently misunderstood. Children near the ends of the normal continuum are often stigmatized, ostracized, or teased. A much more successful way of dealing with the problem is to teach to the needs of the children, without the same expectations in time and content as you have for the others. You have to take the children as far and as quickly as you can, knowing that they may not achieve the same amount of learning. It is important that what they do learn is based upon a solid foundation. Going slowly and sending the children on to others, who also teach for a solid base, will result in more long-term education. It also prevents a lot of frustration because the students did not get the material the first, second, or even third quick time around.

Their behaviors may be acceptable or they may be frustrating. The children may be charming, nice, pretty, blah, or obnoxious. Some are children who frequently have the reputations of "cute but dumb," while others may have little to endear them to us, not even their appearance. They are our students, however, and they must be taught. A positive attitude on our part can help the children accept the fact that they can learn. It's up to us to discover how much.

INTERFERING BEHAVIORS

Most of the behaviors discussed earlier have been the result of some type of prenatal or postnatal medical conditions. Many of the problems that give the classroom teacher the greatest amount of difficulty are behavioral in nature, and they may or may not have a physical basis. Sometimes physicians will medicate children to aid in their behavior management. Those methods will not be discussed here, other than to say that they can be extremely effective in some conditions and useless in others. Since the use of some of the medications is controversial, it is best to make sure that the children have good medical care and then to follow the advice of their doctors. Managing interfering behavior within the classroom will be covered when discussing the tasks we want to teach (Part III) and the settings in which we teach them (Part IV). For now, we merely want to mention the behaviors that the children may bring to you as part of their backgrounds, personalities, and physical make-up.

One of the most disturbing behaviors to bring into a well-established class is that of distractibility. Distractibility may take several different forms. Certain children may have extremely short attention spans. Anything at all can get them off target. Someone across the room dropping a pencil can interrupt their completing their seatwork. The hands on the clock moving and making a slight click can interfere with or break their attention span. They may have such poor powers of concentration that they cannot focus enough to prevent the distractions from interfering with work that has been assigned. Such children may be unable to concentrate on seatwork when there is another group doing oral reading, or unable to work at the science center because they are distracted by what is going on at the reading center.

Hyperactivity is another behavior that causes teachers considerable grief. Such hyperactivity is an increase in motor activity that is disproportionate to the stimulation that set it off. The children may not be able to sit long, attend to a topic for any period of time, and may exhibit erratic and inappropriate behavior on seemingly little provocation. Hyperactive and distractible children are often the ones who leave their seats frequently, interfere with the children around them, talk out in class, and so forth. They may demonstrate impulsive behaviors, not thinking of the consequences of their actions. Some of these impulsive behaviors may lead to other children being hurt in the process. A poke, shove, or jab can lead to damage if committed when the other students are in a vulnerable position or if the hand administering them contains a sharp or dangerous instrument. Such impulsivity may be accompanied by poor judgment. One example comes to mind in which one such child wondered if a paper cutter would cut material. Told by another child to "Try it and find out," he proceeded to cut the collar off a third child's winter coat. When asked why he did it, he replied that the second child had told him to and seemed unaware that he should show remorse for the behavior.

These children may also be poorly organized, not knowing where or how to begin a task. Children demonstrating these behaviors may not complete their work within the allotted time, be unable to follow directions, be purposeless in their activities and behavior, may lose the place in the textbook they are reading, or lose their papers before they are turned in. Such children may build up an expectancy of failure because their behavior has often made them fail in the past. "I can't" or "I'm no good" may be a pervasive attitude. A history of past failure or of uneven performance—when they are able to perform one day and the next day have forgotten everything that's been taught—may result in children who are unable to tolerate failure. They may not even attempt new activities because they are so afraid of failure.

Some of your students may exhibit perseverative behavior, behavior which is continued long after it has lost its meaning. Some children may notice a small speck or imperfection in their notebook paper and proceed to draw circles around it. Before the action is completed, the circle may grow to cover the entire page, totally obliterating the work that has been done previously. Lines may not stop under the words to be underlined, but may continue across the page. As far as knowing when to stop is concerned, such children seem to be unable to control their own behavior. Only when someone else enters in to help are they able to cease their activities. Some children may even cry or become upset when made to stop.

Irritability may be demonstrated by some of these children. A glance by a child sitting in an adjacent seat may evoke an outburst. A mere look may provoke a pounce by the offended children. Again, the behavior that is elicited is out of proportion to the stimulus given.

Motor awkwardness may also be exhibited. As you watch such children walk down the hall, you observe that they may be close to one wall at times and close to the opposite wall at others. Crossing a walking board may be a difficult task. Overflow activities such as the hands flapping while they walk may be seen. Movements of the hands and arms while engaged in gross motor movements with the feet may be observed. Such overflow may also be noted when children stick out their tongues when they write, cut, color, or use any concentration for fine motor movement. Some children may be destructive to toys and to school materials. You may have used particular learning materials for many years, but one usage by one of these children may bring to an end their usefulness. Sturdy construction, plastic covered cards and reading materials, and "indestructible" toys are needed for such children.

Some of these children may get into a lot of difficulty because of their trusting natures. They are indeed guileless and can easily be led into difficulty. These are the children who can be told by a group of children to "Go do____." The specified task is usually prohibited in that setting, and the group lacks the courage to go against the rules. The trusting child merely needs to be told by the group members that "It's all right" to commit the act. This trusting nature, impulsivity, and distractibility, when put in various combinations, can result in frequent conflict with teachers, fellow students, parents, and society in general. Surveys of juvenile offenders show a disproportionate number for which similar behaviors have resulted in brushes with the law.

There is a disparity between the potential for functioning and the actual performance exhibited by such children. These are the children who drive us teachers to distraction! We expect them to be capable students. Their performances are far below that of which we think they're capable, however. We mull over their behavior, wondering how we might reach them, motivate them, prod them. There is frequently a social immaturity which makes the children seem much younger than they really are. Inconsistency in behavior may be demonstrated by very mature behavior in one area and immaturity in others where we would least expect it.

There may be an inability to adjust to new situations. This is often evidenced when teachers are absent and a substitute takes over the classroom. The children may function very well when we are present—when there is a regular schedule that is adhered to—but our absence or a change in schedule because of an assembly, fire drill, or class field trip can result in totally inappropriate behavior.

A bravado may cover a lack of ability. Frequently the children have been retained in a grade, and they may be larger than the other children in the class. This bravado often matches their bigger size, and the other children may be misled by the false bravado, allowing those exhibiting this behavior to become the class bullies. Once that bravado is broken, however, the children are often the objects of taunts and ridicule.

They may also display an inability to delay gratification. Stars, smiling faces, and free time have no meaning for such children, unless delivered simultaneously with the desired behavior, for the children want their rewards *now*. This makes it extremely difficult to work toward long-term goals—the class play at the end of the month, the field trip next week, the party at Halloween. These children have to be very carefully taught to delay gratification; they haven't learned it previously.

Formal tests may show a scatter between the subtests of achievement scores. Testing may be difficult for the children, and the results may not show their true ability. The impulsivity, perseveration, short attention spans, and other behaviors may prohibit them from attending to and carrying out the examiner's directions. A delay in mental processing may also be reflected. One child answered each question only after the next question had been asked. It took that long for him to register the question and give a verbal response. Other children respond, not to the questions, but to the ideas that those questions have generated, thus giving totally inaccurate and inappropriate statements. It is no wonder, then, that the scores fail to reflect their true abilities.

These children may also have difficulties with academic material. Reading problems are not unusual. There may be very poor comprehension of that which has been read. There may also be a problem generalizing material that has been learned. The children may be able to perform in the regular class with the routine materials, but new materials or a new setting may result in their acting as if they had never heard of the facts they know well in the structured setting.

Lack of generalization may also present a problem with behavior that has been taught. For example, the teacher may tell Billy that he is not to take John's pencil after a problem has arisen because he took a pencil from John's desk. This does not prevent Billy from immediately taking a pencil from Sue's desk. Billy has been unable to generalize the fact that he should not take anyone's materials away from them without permission. The teacher has to remember this inability of the children to generalize and so must directly teach generalization to them. Most of the children in the class have the ability to pick up much of their information and generalization skills incidentally, without formal teaching. Those children for whom it remains a problem will have to be specifically taught.

There are other behaviors that may be exhibited by some children. There may be a limited range of interests or an inability to evaluate efforts. Sometimes the children will crumple up a page of acceptable work and replace it with an inferior paper and not know that the second paper is inferior. They may lack common knowledge related to morals, courtesy, and may miss cues from the environment that would allow them to know that their behavior is unacceptable. The open mouth or wide facial expression that alerts others to the fact that they have committed a faux pas means nothing to them.

They may have a limited and crude sense of humor. Someone falling may elicit a great laugh, even if the person is hurt in the process. Some of the children may request frequent help from their teachers, demanding a disproportionate amount of the teacher's time. They may not be aware of the fact that the teacher and the children are reacting negatively to such behavior. There may be a great sense of loyalty in the children, almost of a puppy dog nature. Passing to the next class can be traumatic. Each day after school they may return to your classroom to tell you that they liked your room better than the room in which they are now placed. Next year, however, they will go through the same process with their new teacher.

These, then, are some of the behaviors that children may present to you as a teacher. Their parents' reactions to these behaviors during their preschool years, their friends' reactions, and those of the teachers before you have all influenced the behaviors the children bring to you.

CHAPTER 9
COMMUNICATION PROBLEMS

We have discussed problems of auditory acuity and problems of communication that such acuity losses can bring about. Many children have problems communicating with others despite the fact that there is nothing wrong with their auditory acuity. Because communication problems are so pervasive in children who have hearing losses, the first step usually taken when there are communication problems is to test the children's hearing to rule out an acuity loss. Communication losses can be in the area of written, spoken, or manual language.

Here we will discuss communication problems in the area of spoken language. To have a problem in this area, the traditional definition has been that the speech must call attention to itself, interfere with communication with others, and/or make the user maladjusted because of the problem.

Speech problems are usually of four types: articulation, rhythm, voice, or language. Children may present a single type of communication problem, or they may have a few too many difficulties in each of the separate speech areas. The nature of the handicap can range from minimal to profound, in which there is a total lack of ability to respond verbally.

ARTICULATION ERRORS

Articulation problems result because there are omissions, substitutions, distortions, or additions of the sounds in the words produced. Thus, the child who says *tat* for *cat* has substituted a *t* for a *k* sound, just as the *d* in *yeddow* is a substitution for the *l* in *yellow*. An omission is when the child leaves out sounds, such as *mou* for *mouse* or *tea er* for *teacher*. Distortions result when the children do not make their sounds in quite the usual manner, and the sounds do not come out clearly and understandably. Various types of lisps can be a distortion. We, as Americans, usually distort the French *r* when we speak that language. To a midwesterner, it sounds as if those from Boston distort the *r*, just as the midwestern *r* sounds distorted to one raised in

Boston. Regional accents are not dealt with as communication problems, however, unless they meet the criteria given above as necessary for a speech defect.

The addition of sounds can also be labeled a speech problem. *Spaghetti* is frequently added to by young children, with *spasghetti* resulting. Depending upon the location in the word, the addition of sounds can often distort the word enough so that the word is not understood.

Many articulation problems are a result of immature fine muscle control of the articulators. Speech therapists of preschool children do not usually work on the formation of specific sounds because of this. However, by school age, children should be able to produce correctly most of their sounds, and so articulation therapy may be begun with those sounds that should have been attained by that age.

Some children have many articulation problems and their speech be unintelligible. These children begin speech work early, not so much because they're capable of careful muscular control for good articulation, but to prevent the emotional problems that often accompany speech problems. Speech and language stimulation are given in hopes that the children will be able to take advantage of them and that such stimulation will enable them to speak more clearly. Some of the older children may have had speech therapy for many years, beginning in the preschool years, and still exhibit unintelligible speech. Sometimes this relates to the poor motor control that is shown in other conditions, such as the cerebral palsy we've discussed previously. The children are unable to control the fine motor movements that are needed to have good speech. Other children may have had poor environmental models, have lacked appropriate experiences, or have been conditioned to "be quiet" or "shut up" from an early age.

DISORDERS OF RHYTHM

Another type of speech problem is that of rhythm. We all have breaks in the rhythm of our speech. If we have recorded and then listened to our own voices, we are disturbed with the numbers of *uhs*, *you knows*, and *huhs* that disrupt the influency. This break in fluency is usually normal. It is when it is so great that it interferes with communication that it is recognized as a communication disorder. Since young children in particular have disfluencies, it is important not to make a great issue over them. It is when the children begin to react to the disfluencies by hesitating to speak, or by blinking, forcing speech, footstamping, and so on, that help should certainly be sought.

Stuttering, stammering, repetitions, and forcing speech all are examples of problems with the rhythm of speech. Although there are many theories of the causes of these problems, there is no one particular cause that can be pointed to, and there is no easy cure. Because the degree of disfluency may differ from time to time, pupils with periods of fluency may think they are "cured." This fact may make it particularly difficult to get them to work on their speech when they are less fluent; they are always waiting for a permanent cure and can't see the necessity of working hard to control their periods of disfluency.

The periods of disfluency may vary from a mere repetition of the initial sounds of some words to a complete blockage of speech so that no sounds can come out. The students' reactions to the problems will have much to do with the amount of speaking children are willing to do in your classroom. If the atmosphere is an accepting one and the child is fairly sure of understanding, the amount of communication may be equal to the other children in the class. If, however, the words do not come and the result is embarrassment on the children's part and a lack of communication between you and the child, there may be very little speech. Getting those children to respond in class is a very difficult problem.

VOICE DISORDERS

Voice disorders also call attention to themselves in that the voices are too high, too low, too gruff, too soft, too loud, too nasal, and so forth. Although we all have periods when our voices fall into these categories, the children who have voice disorders sound that way all the time. Some may always sound as if they have cheered themselves hoarse at a football game. Others may have such tiny voices that you may wonder if they could make themselves heard if they had to call for help. Still others sound as if they're talking through their noses. The voices remain that way. Some voice disorders result from physical problems, such as cleft palate. Others may result from misuse of the voice. Any child in the room who has such a voice should be referred for an examination by the speech therapist assigned to your building.

LANGUAGE FUNCTIONING DISORDERS

Disorders of language functioning are found in children who have no speech long past the period of time that children usually start talking. Delayed speech results in a lot of anxiety for parents. Some children who do not talk at the "average" time are merely those within the wide range of normal. They may even be reflecting a family tendency to "talk late." Others may be retarded in development, and speech is one of many indicators of slow development. A few may have the skills to talk but are emotionally disturbed to the degree that they deliberately refuse to speak. Many parents do not know that there are speech clinics available for testing such children to see if there is a real problem or if it is a matter of maturity and the child is merely slow in achieving this skill.

Some people with language problems may be echolalic, merely echoing the words people say to them. They are capable of using all of their articulators appropriately, but spontaneous speech is lacking. Other children may be extremely talkative but the content may be confused and cover many subjects in a very brief period of time. For example, one first grader got up to contribute to "Show and Tell." He began by stating that he had a new puppy. He started to tell how he took the puppy for a walk, but when he began to talk of walking along the water, he soon switched to discussing a ride on a boat that had nothing to do with the puppy he originally started to discuss. This type of language problem is not unusual, and it may be difficult to determine what the children are trying to communicate to you because of it. Such children should be referred for speech therapy.

We have many children now in our school systems who are non-English speaking or limited in their use of English. These children should be referred as language problems. If the children have not been exposed to standard American English in their homes or neighborhoods, enrolling them in a school program in which all instruction is in that language can result in them being thought to be retarded, disturbed, slow-learning, and so forth. The authors of P.L. 94–142 were aware of the large numbers of such children who had been so labeled in the past. They were also aware of some of these children who were labeled and schooled as retarded children who later, after having gained facility with the English language, showed themselves to be gifted rather than retarded. Thus, the section mandating testing for special education placement purposes to be in the children's primary language was included as part of the law.

Children who do not have facility in the language in which they are being taught should be referred for help. If you, as the children's teacher, do not have bilingual abilities, the children should have resource or itinerant help so that your teaching will be successful. Communication between you and the children is imperative.

Another type of language problem is that of aphasia. This is a very complicated language problem, and children who demonstrate the problem to a serious degree will not usually be found in the regular classroom. However, all of us present this problem to some degree, and so we should discuss it. Minor forms of the condition will probably be found within our classes.

This language problem is found in the children's receptive, inner, and/or expressive language functioning. A problem in the receptive area means the children are not receiving the message correctly. It's similar to the poor phone connection in which you can hear people talking but the distortion prevents you from interpreting the message. The children don't understand what is being said to them. The children who have blank looks on their faces and ask us to repeat everything may be demonstrating a form of aphasia. Repetition of the message and use of different vocabulary may make it possible for the receiver to process the message, although it's not that simple with children who have a serious receptive aphasia.

A problem in the inner language area keeps the children from correctly interpreting the message even though the reception of the language is all right. This is similar to hearing a command given to us in an unfamiliar foreign language. We cannot carry out the command because the words hold no meaning for us. And so it is with aphasic children who have a central processing difficulty—words don't have meanings.

A problem in the expressive area is very different from the other two. These children are able to take in the message correctly and to process it properly. They cannot, however, respond expressively to that message. Not only is speech affected, but other areas of expressive language—writing, reading, and spelling—are also affected. It's much like losing our voices completely but also our ability to write out our messages. We can still understand what is said, but we have no way to express ourselves regarding the subject. Our momentary loss of a word we want and the inability to recall familiar names are examples of aphasiclike behavior.

Very serious cases of aphasia may have combined receptive, inner, and expressive language problems. These children present a real challange to educators because of the importance language plays in the educational process. They will not be found in the regular classrooms until they learn to make use of language as a communication tool.

As you can see, there can be a great deal of diversity among the children who are labeled as having communication problems. They will not all have the same amount of interference in their communication with others. The degree of communication difficulties and the willingness to communicate may differ among the children and may be inversely related to the degree of handicap in their speech. Some children who have great disfluencies in speech and severe articulation problems may be great talkers, often driving you to distraction trying to figure out how to understand them enough to communicate with them. Others with very minimal problems may be very reluctant to talk in public because they have been made fun of in the past, or have had difficulty in making someone understand. Usually, however, the more that the speech problems interfere with others' understanding what is being said, the greater the reluctance to speak out. The ones who need the greatest amount of practice are usually the ones who use their speech the least.

CHAPTER 10
ADAPTING TO THE CHILDREN

As we have seen, the problems among the children who are mainstreamed into our classrooms vary in degree and kind. The important thing is that the children are there, and their impairments need to be recognized. The more we are aware of the problems and deal with them in a rational unemotional manner, the more the children can learn to accept their own difficulties, the better their attitude toward school and learning, and the better models we provide for the nonhandicapped children in our classrooms.

The more we know about the handicapping conditions and the functioning of the children the better we will be able to deal with them in the classroom. Following are some ideas that have worked in the past to help children be accepted for what they are—children who are children but who happen to have some type of disability that prevents them from functioning as other, nonhandicapped people function. Although the ideas are written with specific handicaps in mind, it is important to remember that the techniques can often be used with other kinds of handicapping conditions, as well as with your nonhandicapped children.

Faster independence on the part of all the handicapped children will occur if you encourage them to take part in classroom activities, discussions, and leadership roles, just as you do the other children. It is also important that you apply the same methods of discipline to the handicapped children that you do to all your children. To apply different levels of behavioral expectation for the handicapped children is unfair to them. It teaches them that they are special and do not have to obey rules that apply to everyone else. It also makes the other children in the class resentful of the special privileges that are given to the handicapped children. Instead of learning to treat them as equals, they learn to resent the handicapped. If you have any negative feelings about the handicapped children, you will have to monitor your actions carefully to make sure that any feelings of frustration you have about them are not passed on to your class. Nonverbal communication is easily transmitted, and you want to avoid making anyone in the class think that the handicapped children are to be viewed negatively.

73

There are ways in which you can encourage all of the class members to interact with the handicapped children. Having little children take off their hearing aids and show the children how they work and how they sound can do much to end suspicion. An older child can take apart the aid and demonstrate how the circuitry works, how to replace the batteries, or some other appropriate activity for the children of that age.

Races in which each child uses the handicapped child's crutches to race a certain distance can also be effective. The children who have never been on crutches are often much slower because of the practice the handicapped children have had. Or they may notice a pain under their arms because they are not aware of the proper way to use the crutches. This can become an excellent opportunity for the handicapped children to explain their proper use.

A rational, unemotional explanation by the handicapped child about the handicap may do much to dispel fear. One little girl, teased because she "talked funny," let all the children who were in the group look at the hole in the top of her mouth. Her words, "I talk funny because I've got this hole in the top of my mouth," led all the others to look in each others' mouths to see if they had similar holes. Assured that they did not, the matter was dropped and no more teasing occurred.

In one setting, a number of handicapped children were integrated with nonhandicapped children. The class aide, a young girl with a prosthesis, or artificial limb, for her missing arm, asked if she could show how her arm worked when the children in the group refused to take her "hand" during a circle activity in gym. Removing the prosthesis, but not the muscle insertion, she showed the children how she could open and close her hook. All were amazed with this ability. All looked closely at the small rudiments of an arm that she was born with and that she fastened her prosthesis to. When the demonstration was over, one child boldly grabbed her hook. After that, none feared to touch it.

Your unemotional approach will do much to help the children accept the handicapped. For children who have already been instilled with fear, suspicion, or mistrust, a more direct approach may be needed. Interaction with the handicapped can often dispel their fears, and so you need to provide the opportunities for the children to interact. Forming groups that include the handicapped children can help, especially if the group includes a room leader that you know will approach the children on a very unemotional basis. One group was able to accept one child to such a great extent that they chided her for being slow when playing a card game, even though her slowness resulted from her not having the use of the hand that was holding the cards. Her reminder that it took awhile to get the cards out brought all kinds of suggestions from the others as to how she might hold her cards for faster movement.

If you are using the types of classroom peer aides that we will discuss later, these aides can often be assigned to help the handicapped children.

Someone to act as a sighted guide for a blind child or an interpreter to make sure that a deaf child understands what is going on can be assigned from your other children. Older children may want to become advocates for particular children. Some community groups train students in the various types of handicapping conditions and then have them volunteer to be "lookouts" for their handicapped peers. This means that they are responsible for a child assigned to their class in junior or senior high school and look out to see that the children are included in regular school activities. Children who would never have even been included in activities were it not for the lookouts become leaders of groups because their lookouts do such nice jobs of making sure that the other students learn about the real person beneath the handicapping label.

Including the children in boy and girl scout troops, Sunday school groups, youth and hobby groups, and so on, can aid in showing others that they are very normal in their likes and dislikes, personalities, and intellects. Just as with their nonhandicapped peers, some children will be popular and some not. Some will become leaders and not others. All should have the opportunity.

During the teenage years, handicapped children have a particularly difficult time. In a day when teenagers don't want to vary a bit from their peers in the way they look, what they say, how they say it, and so on, children who are different in many ways may be ostracized from the group. If you have tried to get the handicapped children into activities and they seem to be rejected by most of their peers, it may be possible to pair them with other of the peer rejects to form their own little group. Finding something that the children have in common may take a lot of your time, but all children need to be accepted by their peers, and their mainstreamed years will be much happier if they have friends with whom they can share them.

ADAPTING FOR HEARING ACUITY LOSSES

The following are things to remember if some of your students have been evaluated and found to have an auditory acuity loss or if children with hearing handicaps are placed within your class for educational purposes. Children with a hearing loss should be seated close to the teacher in order to hear the maximum that can be obtained through the use of residual hearing. Since most hearing handicapped children, even those with profound losses, are rarely totally deaf, use should be made of what hearing they have left. However, the children will also gain many cues from facial expressions, lips, body language, and so forth, and so it is important to place them so they can use all of these cues. Do not place the children so that they will be looking at your face from an angle, as that will eliminate a lot of cues. Seating yourself at the level of the children may be one way that you can manage to place yourself in full view at least part of each day, particularly until the children become more familiar with your expressions and learn to read them from greater angles of vision. The best seating for the children will be where they can turn to observe the rest of the class and where it is relatively quiet so that background noise will not block out what hearing there is.

It is important for you not only to be at face level while you are talking to them, particularly until they become familiar with your lip movements, but also that you stand in a part of the room where the light falls on your face. Standing against the windows will hide your facial features and make speech reading more difficult. Standing where a light falls directly on your face will aid the children in picking up what you are saying. Lipstick on a woman's lips and the absence of beard or mustache on a man's face will also aid the children.

It is important to remember that the children will be unable to get clues of what you are saying if you speak while writing on the blackboard. You will have to train yourself to write and then turn to speak if you want the deaf children to gain the most of what you are saying. The same thing is true if you talk while you walk around the room. The children need to keep your face always in view if they are to learn maximally. Writing out class assignments will also aid the children to know what is expected. Written assignments lessen the chance of the children's misinterpretation or forgetting what you have spoken.

If you have ever studied a foreign language, the next recommendation should bring back memories. Remember how tired you felt after attending a class in which the teacher lectured only in the foreign language and you were attending to every word that was spoken so as to miss nothing of importance? Or remember taking notes from a professor who lectured very rapidly and gave many facts that were essential to success in the course? Remember how drained you felt at the end of the class period? The same type of response is felt by children with a hearing loss who strain to attend to every word that is spoken during the class period, for the children cannot hear by voice inflection the facts that are emphasized and those that are slighted. A system needs to be developed between you and the children so that they can rest from the constant strain of viewing. Verbal or nonverbal systems can be worked out between you and the children to indicate that something important is coming. They need to know that if they are not being particularly attentive, you will gain their attention.

Because the children will not be able to visually attend to what you are saying and to write at the same time, a class where notetaking is important will be difficult for them. Furnishing carbon and paper to good students who take accurate and lengthy notes will enable those students to share their notes with the hearing handicapped children.

It will probably be necessary for you to work out specific arrangements with each particular child to best aid that child. Placing a question mark on the board each time you ask a question may help. Identifying the source of someone speaking out in the classroom and repeating the spoken question or answer can also aid. Otherwise, the child may be visually scanning the classroom to see the source of sound all the while the question is being answered, thus missing the content. Children in the classroom can be taught to hold their hands up or to stand up while talking so that the hearing impaired child can locate the source of sound quickly.

Because malfunctioning hearing aids often account for some of the deaf children's inability to obtain all they might from an educational environment, each child's aid should be checked each day. There are specific ways to do this, and the itinerant or resource room special education teacher can give particular advice about the way this can be undertaken. However, the children should assume responsibility for the operation of their own aids. Parents can be of help with this if the children are young. By knowing the way in which the children have been taught to check for such things as battery failure, cord breaks and connections, and wax in the earmold, you can aid them by reminding them daily, if necessary, to carry out such activities. Teaching them independence in this activity is just as important to their futures as teaching them the multiplication tables.

All of these things will aid you in helping children with an auditory acuity loss that are placed in your classroom. However, there is a greater task that you must undertake if you are to be an effective teacher with hearing impaired children. You must always keep in mind the tremendous language handicaps that children with severe and profound hearing losses have. Our language is particularly complex, and if we fail to keep this in mind, we will do an injustice to the children we are attempting to aid.

Let's use just one example to illustrate the complexity that a child who will never hear the spoken word might have in learning a word as simple as *catch*. We normally think of the expression "catch a ball" as illustrative of the word. This would be easy to demonstrate to deaf children to enable them to have an idea of the meaning of the word. Yet we do not catch a cold in that manner. Nor do we catch a fish by holding out our hands. There are many other uses of the word catch that might further confuse the meaning of the word for the children. We catch our clothes on a nail, a catch closes a door, we might catch you with the evidence, or catch you in the act. We can catch up with you, or catch a train, but not with our hands. We also might catch ourselves doing something, catch the spirit of something, or catch a movie. We know that wood catches fire, that we catch on to an idea, catch our breath, catch someone when we become engaged, catch ourselves from falling, and catch an error we made. We really catch it if we do something wrong and someone finds out about it. We hope to catch up with our bills, we get a catch in our throats, and that may catch attention. There are probably many more if we stop to think of them.

A problem arises because the children will eventually have to learn all of the proper uses of this one word. We must then multiply that problem by all of the words that the children must learn to be a member of our literate society. Although the task seems overwhelming, it can be put simply: a teacher who undertakes the education of deaf children must constantly be ready to interpret, reinforce meanings, and alert children to old as well as new vocabulary words. Words must be reviewed periodically to see if the meanings are still retained. New meanings for old words need to be introduced.

Each time you introduce a new word or new meaning, a way to help you remember to review the words is to write the word in the margin beside your lesson plans for the week. Then throughout the next few days you can make sure you review the word each day in some manner. The next week write the word in the margin for review every other day. The following couple of weeks do it once. Then write, at random, the vocabulary word in the margin beside a number of weeks. As you go through your lesson plans each week and see that word in the margin, it will remind you to include it in your lessons that week.

To be an effective teacher of hearing handicapped children one must be part actor and very creative. Constant reinforcement of prior learning is necessary. Only by doing it can one see the response—the sudden recognition that shows on the children's faces when presented with what was thought to be a new word, or the carefully written paper that shows the attainment of knowledge. Teaching such children is not easy, but it certainly can be rewarding.

ADAPTING FOR VISUAL ACUITY LOSSES

Dealing with students who have visual acuity problems presents a different kind of challenge. There may be children in your class who were placed there after they were found to be visually impaired. You may have several questions about what you should be doing to make sure that they have the best type of education you can give them. Most of these questions can be answered by the vision specialist who will be assigned to work with you and the children. This specialist will be able to provide the types of special materials the children need because of their visual problems. This person will also be able to answer specific questions that you have about the particular visual problems that the children possess. In time, and with age, the children themselves should be able to provide the types of information needed and will be able to give you specific guidelines for helping them. Young children will necessitate that more information be provided by the vision specialist or parent, but the children should all be encouraged to learn about their own problems and be able to communicate their needs and information about their eye conditions to others.

As mentioned before, there is no correlation between the amount of residual vision children have and the way in which that vision is used. Two children with the same eye problem and visual acuity may be very different in their visual utilization. Fatigue, lighting, and emotions may effect the use children make of their limited vision. Thus, it is very difficult to make blanket recommendations for ways that children should be treated in the regular classroom. However, there are some general conditions that will apply to all of the children.

Don't be afraid to use the words "look" and "see" when talking with the children, even those who have no vision at all. The children have probably heard these words throughout their lives, and the words should be a part of their regular vocabulary. Although persons with vision use these words in a different context, the visually impaired persons will be able to tell from their use that they must either tactually or visually closely examine the objects that are being discussed. Thus, the object that you have brought for the class to "see" becomes an object for the totally blind children to investigate with their hands.

You will also want to include the visually handicapped children in all of the activities in which your class takes part. The vision teacher will have specific means, equipment, or techniques to offer in helping you to teach the children. There is no reason why all the children can't participate in shop, home economics, and gym when using these techniques. Although there may be particular restrictions placed on some eye conditions, there is no reason why the children cannot partake in all activities for which they have a doctor's clearance.

Children who have limited vision may have difficulty in moving around in their environment. Although it is much easier to let the visually limited children sit and to bring needed materials to them, such efforts will prevent them from becoming as independent as possible. The children need to learn to move about. They need to learn that the world is not brought to them, but that they must go out and seek what they want. Only then will they learn the techniques to succeed in our modern competitive society.

When first placed in your room, visually handicapped children should be exposed to the arrangement of the room by the vision teacher and/or orientation and mobility instructor. (Some teachers are dually trained, or you might have two specific people assisting your student.) After the children have become familiar with the room layout, it will be necessary to let them know each time you rearrange any furniture. Major rearrangements may necessitate a completely new room orientation.

The children should be allowed a particular place for the many materials that are needed by the visually limited. Braille books are extremely bulky, as are large-print texts. Reading stands, viewers, magnifiers, recorders, and so forth, may need particularly secure and safe storage. Additional work space may be needed by the children to spread out their materials, to use the readers, and to have room to use braille books and braillers. Enough space to ensure that the children will be able to function adequately is imperative.

Many children are very self-conscious of their need for aids and adaptations, and some children may be very reluctant to use them. Your very open acceptance of the children and of the materials and equipment will do much to set the tone and example for the rest of the group. Sometimes letting other children view objects by using the aids, explaining the braille alphabet, and attempting to use the brailler will do much to help them understand the problems visually impaired children have in coping with their materials. The children may gain new respect from their peers because they are able to use machines that appear very complicated to the non-impaired children.

It is important that the children in the classroom learn to identify themselves by name when approaching a child with a severe visual problem. Sometimes the visually handicapped children are described as "stuck-up" or "snooty" when they are unable to identify voices from around them and are reluctant to reply to voices that come at them from out of nowhere. Again, by setting an example and identifying yourself, the children will learn to do the same until the voices become familiar.

There will be times when the visually limited children in your classroom will need you to act as a sighted guide. The specialist for the visually handicapped will be of help in showing particular techniques for searching, guiding, seating, and so forth. The children themselves may be able to aid you with these techniques if they have already been taught them. To use the guiding technique, the children should grasp your upper arm, just above the elbow, with the thumb on the outside and the fingers on the inside of your arm. Young children may grasp your waist if they are too short to grab your upper arm. By grabbing your arm in that position, the visually handicapped children will be in a position one-half step behind you. By being this half-step behind, the children will have time to adjust their steps for avoiding obstacles. By moving your arm behind your body, you alert the children to move directly behind you as you move through narrow openings and doorways.

All of the children in the class can be taught the techniques for being sighted guides to their classmate. The vision specialist assigned to assist you with the children in your class will be able to instruct both you and the children. Again, your attitude toward the children and the techniques that must be used for them to adapt to their environment will do much to set an example for the children in your classroom.

Sometimes young children are amazed that blind children are able to navigate in their environment. The children may walk around the room with their eyes closed when a blind child first enters the classroom. Teachers may be concerned with this imitation, afraid that the children will hurt themselves. Such imitation soon loses its appeal, and the children quickly lose interest once they learn that they, too, can move in their surroundings without harm. Some of the children are surprised that the blind youngsters are able to feed themselves without vision and do not realize that none of us see the mouths into which we push our food.

It is usually wise to let the children carry out these activities. They usually quell much of the curiosity and may actually build an admiration for the children without vision. All of this, if handled without emotion, can aid the children in their acceptance of the visually handicapped people they will meet in their lifetimes.

The eye conditions hyperopia and myopia present a challenge to teachers in the early elementary classes. The teachers of kindergarten and first and second grades have to be very careful in the observation of the children in these classes to pick out problems children may be exhibiting. No children of this age should be required to spend great amounts of time using their eyes in close work, especially with regular-sized print that requires a lot of accommodating on the part of the muscles that change the shape of the lens so that it can focus the light rays onto the retina. If the children are greatly hyperopic, they may not be aware of discomfort, but will often become fidgety, restless, rub their eyes, and show great resistance to the types of activities that require close work.

Children who are myopic, on the other hand, will show no such resistance to close work and, in fact, will enjoy it. Those particular children, because they will not be able to see at distances, may prefer reading and other close work to playing outside on the playground. This is because the eyes are quite comfortable doing close work, while carrying out a game of catch can result in discomfort. The children may not be able to focus on the ball coming at them until it is too late. This may result in the children being hit on the ends of the fingers or on the head by the ball because of the delay in visual then motor response. It would be interesting to know how often sports have become aversive to myopic children because they resulted in early injuries or pain. It would also be interesting to know how many behavior problems have been caused because children were forced to sit in their seats and read small print under a constant strain, forcing their eyes to accommodate to read the letters. Some children may take on the role of the class clown or the class dummy as an alternative to remaining seated and continuing an uncomfortable activity.

The ability of children to use their near vision to the maximum is often interfered with because of the misinformation that we were fed during our formative years. Our parents often told us not to hold the books so close to our eyes, that we'd hurt them if we did. We were told not to read in dim light because we'd ruin our eyes. We were told that there was a certain manner in which we were supposed to handle our papers and our books so that we would not become blind. These prejudices and unfounded statements often became a part of our thinking and we end up passing on the misinformation. Thus, it is important to remember that there is no evidence that holding material close will ruin the eyes. Nor are there data that show use of the eyes in dim light will hurt them. Although there supposedly is a maximum point for comfort at which the printed page should be held away from the eyes, this distance is based upon what the normal eye is capable of perceiving. Because we know that "normal" has a wide range there will be some variation between what some people find comfortable and what others are able to tolerate.

Sometimes students must have magnifiers or other types of visual aids to help them see the printed page comfortably. Others are able to let the eyes make their adjustments for them and are able to read by bringing the printed page closer to the eyes. If children are able to read in this manner, there is no reason that they should not be allowed to do it.

Visually impaired children should be encouraged to place the material they are using at whatever distance they find comfortable to read. The arms are the best visual aids we have, in that we can bring things as close as or extend them as far away as we need them. Children may bring materials right up to their faces, while we who are older may place the material farther and farther from the eyes. How often have we seen someone hold a needle out at arm's length from the eyes while attempting to thread it? As we get older, the eyes lose their ability to accommodate. That means that the eyes cannot adjust as easily between things that are far and near. Thus we use our arms to bring things closer or farther away. As we age, the loss is great enough so that lenses need to be placed in front of the eyes to aid in the accommodation. The children in your room are doing essentially the same thing. The children's lenses do not allow enough accommodation to read the letters, and so they aid the lenses by bringing the material closer for the eyes to see.

Research shows that the use of the eyes alone will do no damage to them, except in very rare instances of particular eye problems. Thus, use of the eyes is good. The more the children use their eyes to interpret what is around them, the more they will be able to use them. They will learn more and more about their environment and be able to relate to it much more effectively. It may be necessary for them to "eyeball" certain things or to "nose read" to make sense of the printed page. These activities in themselves will do no harm to the children's vision. If that is what the children must do to read, they should be allowed to do it. Constant reminders to hold the book farther away from the eyes or to "sit up straight" will mean that you are taking from the children the only means they have for seeing the printed page. Instead, types of adaptive equipment, such as book holders that angle reading material so that children can comfortably get close to it, should be given to them.

If expenses prevent you from having such aids in the classroom, a book support can be constructed from a corrugated cardboard box and a paring knife from the kitchen. By cutting a flat piece of cardboard and folding it into three pieces to form a triangle—and then cutting the one end so that there are tabs on it and slitting places in the other end for the pieces to fit through—a very serviceable book holder can be made. By making the tabs wide and long enough so that several inches extend through the slits, a book can be supported on the protruding tabs. If you feel that children are not using the aid because it calls attention to the fact that they are "different," such bookholders can be constructed for the whole class. These can sometimes be constructed in an art class by children old enough to use the knives necessary for their construction, or they may be produced by a girl or boy scout troop or some type of service agency that is willing to donate the time and effort needed to construct them.

You can support the children's efforts to make the print easier to see by not drawing attention to or attempting to correct their posture or the distance at which they hold their books. You can also help the children by listening for any remarks that other children might make and explaining why the visually handicapped children are using the material they are, thus taking away the emotional issues involved. Since young children often verbally attack what is new or different or what is unknown to them, an unemotional discussion as to why it is necessary for some people to hold their books in different positions can do much to alleviate any teasing that may take place. A teaching unit on vision can be used with older children as part of their health, science, or biology classes. Ignorance is often a cause of mistrust and emotionalism. Education can do much to dispel it. A calm, unemotional approach is necessary, and if you feel insecure in dealing with the topic, it may be better for you to ask the support personnel in vision to aid you in these endeavors. That's part of their purpose for being there.

ADAPTING FOR MOTOR IMPAIRMENTS

Cerebral palsy can take many forms and may involve only a small part of the body or it may affect the total motor movements of the children. If only one arm, one leg, or one side (hemiplegia) of the body is involved, few adaptations may need to be made in the classroom. Your major task will be to see that the children use both sides of their bodies. Otherwise, the affected limbs will atrophy, contract, and be of even less use. Activities that demand the use of both hands or legs are excellent, in that the children will have to use the involved limbs.

If, however, both legs (paraplegia) or both hands and both legs (quadriplegia) are involved, some means will have to be provided for the children to move about. This may involve crutches if the children are able to maintain their balance and manipulate the crutches, or it may involve a wheelchair. The wheelchairs may be propelled by the children if there is enough ability to do it, or it may be necessary to have a motorized wheelchair if the children do not have the movement or stamina to manipulate the chair. Some children have such involvement in their limbs that others will have to push them. The normal classroom peers are usually most anxious to operate wheelchairs of both types and may have a great respect for the ability of those who are able to operate them appropriately. One precaution that should be taken when wheelchairs are involved is to make sure that the brakes are set on both wheels whenever the chair is not in motion. Set brakes are particularly important whenever transfer from the wheelchair is made. Serious accidents can be prevented by this means.

One of the classroom concerns when dealing with motorically handicapped children usually involves where to store the walkers or crutches while the children are seated in the classroom. A place out of the way of the other children but readily available to the handicapped children is necessary. Placing the walker directly beside, in front of, or in back of the desks is most preferable because the children can readily obtain them for independent mobility. Hooks such as those used to hold brooms and mops can be attached to the backs of the desk chairs to keep the crutches out of the way of the other children and yet still be readily available.

Classroom adaptations for the children may be as minimal as taping their papers to the table so that their papers won't slide and they are able to use all their energies to write. Or it may mean that head sticks must be attached to a band around the children's heads so that they can operate electric typewriters on which a special template has been placed to prevent several keys from being pressed at one time. Obviously, those in need of the former adaptation will need no extra space around them, while those who need the latter will require room for the typewriter, books, headstick, and so forth. The needs of the children will determine the amount of space needed for their mobility and adaptive equipment.

There are many manufacturing companies in this country whose sole purpose is to produce adaptive equipment for the use of physically handicapped people. The catalogs alone from such companies would fill several file drawers. Certain kinds of equipment will be useful for just about any problem your children with motor problems might have. It is not up to you alone to determine the types of equipment they might need, however.

Physical and occupational therapists, along with special educators, will discuss with you the needs of the specific children. If you have concerns about the children's needs for some type of adaptive equipment, voice these concerns about these resources. The educator is usually concerned with the educational aspects, while the therapists are concerned with normal or adaptive movements. Because the goal of these people is to make the handicapped children as able to function in the least restrictive setting as possible, they will choose adaptive equipment on that basis. In other words, there may be some types of equipment that may be constructed for the types of problems that your children are exhibiting but the equipment would make the children less able to attend a regular classroom. They might choose not to obtain the equipment because of it. Or, they may want the children to learn how to adapt to available equipment rather than to some type of special equipment. An example is the use of adapted silverware. It is readily available and relatively inexpensive. However, children who are dependent on such adaptations are less able to eat with their peers in the school cafeteria or to go to the nearest snack bar with their buddies after the school day is over. One child we know threw a complete school into pandemonium because her adapted silverware disappeared when the lunch dishes were washed. She had never learned to eat without them and insisted she'd go without her dinner rather than eat without them. (She didn't.)

Some adaptive equipment is unnecessary and calls attention to the fact that the users are different. Those who are familiar with the children and their needs should be the ones to evaluate them for their need for adaptive equipment. Whenever you have motorically handicapped children in your classroom, you should immediately contact the physical and occupational therapists to obtain from them the things you will need to know about positioning, carrying, lifting, and so forth. Some children who have a lot of extension in their body movements will literally be unable to move themselves when placed in certain positions. The therapists can demonstrate the right kinds of positions, and you should practice using them while the therapists are still there. This will give you greater confidence when you are alone.

Remember that if you need to lift the children for any reason, the lifting should be done with the large leg muscles, not the back. Remembering this fact will keep you from having back problems. The therapists will remind you of this, but it is something that teachers often forget.

If you can get the therapists to do some of their work within the confines of your classroom, you will be able to observe what they are doing and be able to carry it out when they are not present. Sometimes the limited time devoted to therapy can be better spent in instructing you how to implement what is needed than it is in direct therapy with the children.

The special educator or speech therapist will be able to help you with nonverbal children whose motor problems keep them from communicating verbally. Because of the great numbers of communication devices that are available for the children to use, it is important to evaluate which ones are the most appropriate for particular children. Once they have established which ones are the most effective, you need to learn to operate the devices yourself so that you know how the children should be using them. This will also aid you in determining that something is wrong with the devices when they aren't working properly. A nonverbal child may not be able to communicate the fact that something is wrong with a particular device when the device isn't working enough to let the child communicate that fact.

Children who have no feeling in their lower body may be prone to a decubitus, or bed sore. This occurs because there is pressure on the skin and the nerves that usually tell us we have been sitting in one spot too long are not working. The skin may break down, and an open sore can result. Because that part of the body is poorly innervated, the ability of the body to repair itself is impaired. Small sores become larger and deeper. Skin grafts may be necessary in order to repair the damage, and even they may not be effective.

The best way to deal with decubiti is to avoid conditions that make them. The children who have upper arm use can help by lifting their body weight up on their arms and reseating themselves. This will redistribute the body weight and usually prevent a decubitus from forming. Children who do not have the use of their upper arms to lift themselves from their chairs will have to be repositioned in another of the accepted positions given to you by the occupational or physical therapists. Such repositioning should be done each half hour for maximum protection against decubiti and to prevent the muscle contraction that can result if nonmotoric children are left in one position for a long period of time.

A few of the motorically impaired children who are mainstreamed will have eating problems because the muscle problems that caused the motor problems also effect those that help us eat. The occupational, speech, or physical therapist will be able to help you with this. Again, that is what the therapists are there for and their aid will enable the children to remain with their normal peers throughout the rest of the day. Wise use of their skills will help the children and you make mainstreaming even more advantageous.

ADAPTING FOR CHRONIC HEALTH PROBLEMS

As we've said before, chronic health problems differ in kind and in severity. The parents and the school nurse will probably have informed you of the type of health conditions that the children have. They should also have given you basic information in how to deal with specific problems these health conditions might entail. If they haven't, you should request such information.

One subject that invariably arises has to do with medication and whether the teacher should be responsible for its administration. Different schools have different rules regarding this, and so you should find out what your school's are. Some insist teachers not handle the medication in any way, although they do allow the teacher to remind their students when it's time to take it. Some insist that a doctor write a prescription that allows teachers to administer the medication. Others insist the teacher send the children to the school nurse, who administers it. Some schools have no rules, but the teacher unions do. In other schools there are no restrictions. Knowing the particular practices to be followed in your school will allow you to help the children keep their medication schedules.

The easiest way you will feel comfortable in dealing with your student's chronic health problems is to educate yourself to what they are. A list of resources to which you can write can be found in Part V. Say that you are a classroom teacher and that you have students in your class with that particular type of problem. The organizations usually have a list of readings, materials, references, and so on, that they have collected particularly for classroom teachers and will send them to you at little or no cost. Because these organizations want children mainstreamed into the regular classroom as much as possible, they are usually extremely helpful in providing the type of information that will be useful to you. For example, one of the things you might want to do if you have a diabetic child in the classroom is to have a ready source of sugar in your desk. Hard candies or cans of orange juice might be appropriate. Keeping track of a sudden increase of trips to the toilet and drinking fountains might be information that you can provide the doctors. Monitoring seizures, keeping track of antecedent and consequential behaviors, can determine if the child is using seizures to avoid unpleasant tasks. Careful watch for bruises in a hemophiliac should be a matter of fact. Such monitoring might keep the child from an internal bleeding that would have dire outcome if not discovered. Watching the movements of children who have muscular problems, such as a dystrophy, or joint disease, such as Legg Perthe's, can aid in preventing further damage or inappropriate activities being undertaken by the children. By obtaining appropriate literature and learning the essential factors to look for in working with each particular child, you can then direct your efforts to the factors that are critical and can relax and enjoy the children as they interact with others in your classroom.

One way that teachers can become better informed and can aid their students better to understand the other children within their classes is to assign a project or papers on the various types of conditions found within the class. Health class or English classes provide excellent opportunities for the children themselves to look into the literature regarding their own types of handicapping conditions. Science classes, in which recent developments and areas that need further research are discussed, are also appropriate settings for researching topics and discussing their ramifications.

When discussing chronic health problem subjects, care should be taken in the way in which they are presented. It may be very difficult for the students to distinguish between discussing a disease we feel negatively about and looking negatively at the people who happen to possess that disease or condition. Facts about different health conditions should enable you and your students to differentiate between the negative feelings regarding conditions and the feelings about those who have them. Who knows? In your discussions of the various conditions, you may stimulate some child in your class to become so involved in the subject that that child may later make some tremendous contribution with regard to a particular condition.

ADAPTING FOR SLOW LEARNING
AND INTERFERING BEHAVIORS

All children want to communicate and be liked by their teachers. Some go about getting your attention in desirable ways and others will do anything, desirable or not. Your major responsibility in dealing with children with interfering behaviors is to structure the situation so that the children make appropriate responses and you give them the attention that they want as a reward for those appropriate actions. Following are techniques that are appropriate for all of your children. They are essential for slow learners and for those with interfering behaviors.

Consistency

We all seem to hate inconsistency. We become very angry if our bosses tell us to do one thing and later tell us to do another. We become particularly disturbed if the two directions appear to be opposites. We are quick to verbalize our feelings of frustration. These verbalizations may not be directed at the source of our frustrations for fear of some type of reprisal, but our mates, fellow teachers, or friends will know how unhappy we are.

Students, too, have a great dislike for inconsistency. Students who have little ability to organize themselves or their environment are particularly apt to be disturbed by a teacher's lack of consistency. Because they cannot depend on themselves for that consistency, they seek it in others. They may feel their teacher to be the source for consistency, only to become disillusioned when they notice inconsistencies.

Lack of consistency can ruin a behavior management program. Children have a need to know that a teacher means what is said and will stand behind it. One teacher who was having a particularly difficult time maintaining discipline and motivation within his classroom listened carefully to the suggestions of his fellow teachers. He decided to begin a new program that he hoped would result in both behavior changes and attitudinal changes in his students. He carefully outlined the behavioral rules to be followed. He explained acceptable as well as nonacceptable behavior to his students. The program, which lasted for six weeks, seemed to be working. He kept to his rules, and the students carefully followed them, making academic gains while they were purposefully occupied.

At the end of the six-week period, the two students who had had the best behavior were rewarded with large chocolate bars, the promised reward. Because the teacher didn't want the other students disappointed, he gave them all similar chocolate bars. All students, no matter how much or how little they had worked, were rewarded in the same manner. The teacher couldn't understand when he began a similar program two weeks later why the behaviors and attitude were not maintained. None of the students seemed interested in working toward a new reward.

The teacher was not able to see that he had affected all of the children's behavior and attitudes by rewarding them equally, no matter how much work and interest they had invested. Frequent discussions with his fellow teachers didn't seem to clarify the situation. His students' behavior seemed to regress as the year went by. The teacher, who failed to receive a recommendation for contract renewal from the principal and supervisor, was asked to leave the system.

Many teachers have classes that aren't under control, but the children's behavior is not so out of bounds that the teachers' contracts are in jeopardy. Many are borderline, but their supervisors and principals recommend contract renewal, hoping the behavior management skills will improve. Sometimes tenure is given with these same hopes, which never materialize. Thus, teachers may become part of an established system, but may still need skills in classroom management.

Teachers must learn that consistency is a vital part of their classroom management techniques. Students need to learn that teachers mean what they say. Threats and promises mean nothing if students learn that they won't be carried out. If teachers carry out those threats and promises, the children learn that actions will follow words and that the teachers can be depended on to do what they say they'll do. Behavior begins to reflect this knowledge. Because they know that they will have to be carried out, teachers become much more careful in making threats and promises. After we've spent a whole afternoon with a group of children that were denied their recess period because of a rash threat, we cautiously consider threats before we voice them aloud to our students.

The punishment should fit the crime. A minor infraction of some rule should not be punished by a major type of punishment. Students are particularly aware of injustices and are indignant when they occur. Making the whole class stay in from recess because of one child's behavior is apt to lead to punitive actions toward that child by the others, as well as a great deal of resentment toward the teacher whom they feel is unjust.

Modeling

Teachers can do a great deal in establishing the type of behavior they desire in a classroom by calling attention to that behavior when it occurs. "I like the way Jimmy is sitting quietly while we're waiting," is much more effective in getting the children to quiet down than "Johnny, you're making too much noise." The former provides a model for the type of conduct desired. The other children, seeking similar praise, will quickly try to imitate that behavior.

The attitude of the teacher and the example that is set can do much toward setting up a manageable classroom. The teacher who is excited and interested will be more apt to stimulate children than the teacher who is bored, disinterested, lethargic, or fearful of the material. It would be interesting to know the numbers of adults who have been prejudiced against mathematics by teachers who had a particular bias against the subject. Many elementary teachers are not comfortable teaching math and science, and that feeling permeates their teaching, creating students with similar reactions toward those subjects.

How much better a model is the teacher who is enthusiastic about the whole idea of learning. The feeling becomes contagious, and the students quickly become caught up in the spirit. Teachers who are concerned with their effect on their students will present a model they want their students to copy. They will be quick to praise those children who do endeavor to imitate particular behaviors. They will call attention to appropriate responses on the part of their charges, thereby establishing further examples of desired behavior.

Teachers very often fail to respond to or verbally recognize the type of behavior they desire when they see it in their students. Instead, they are more apt to let the good slip by and call attention to the inappropriate. Yet, as adults, we are quick to criticize our administrators for doing the same thing to us. An occasional "pat on the back" will go a long way. We all have a need to be recognized and to be appreciated. "That's a good job," can do much to make an individual child feel good for the day. It can also help the children around that child see an example of what pleases us.

Sometimes students are not sure of what their teachers want, of what criteria will be used to judge their assignments. We've all had that experience in college courses. "Give us an example," becomes a common request. Giving positive feedback to those students who are meeting our criteria helps them as well as those around them to focus on the behavior we want from them. Calling attention to appropriate models can be much more effective than criticizing inappropriate ones. The latter merely lets children know what we don't want, not what it is we're looking for.

It's also important to praise the whole class when they've been behaving as we want them to behave. "I like the way you're working," "You've been such quiet students this morning," and "You've been working so well this morning I thought we might have some free time," are all things students like to hear. The old adage of catching more flies with honey than vinegar is certainly appropriate where classroom management is concerned.

One word of caution is necessary, however, when considering model behavior. It is important that the same child is not always singled out as the appropriate model. A number of children may exhibit the desired behavior, and the praise should go to different ones over time. Otherwise, we end up with the one child who receives a lot of recognition being labeled "teacher's pet." Instead of becoming a model to be followed, this child is more apt to be a target for derision and one who will eventually become ostracized by the other children. All children will exhibit the desired behaviors at some point, and quick recognition of that behavior will reward the child for functioning in that manner as well as point out a model for the others to follow.

Teacher-Child Interaction

Teachers and children need to interact, not just react. Years ago, teachers ordered and students responded. There was little interaction between the two. We now believe that children should gradually become responsible for their own behavior, and our interactions reflect this belief. We now involve the children in decision-making processes to a much greater degree. Students are given choices in activities. They learn to accept some responsibility for activities. They gradually are able, through this process, to become responsible for activities and for their own behavior. This does not occur overnight or automatically. The interaction and development of responsibility must be fostered through careful planning. The teacher's behavior throughout these activities will directly affect the students' eventual behavior.

Students need to know that their teacher likes them and is comfortable in the teaching role. Some teachers are openly affectionate. Others are not. Whether or not you as a teacher are openly affectionate is not the important issue. Rather, it is whether or not you convey to your children the fact that you like them and you like what you are doing. If you don't, you shouldn't be teaching. If you do, there should be some way for you to get this across to your students. Some teachers who are extremely critical of their students and very negative in the classroom actually enjoy what they are doing. It's very difficult to convince their students of this fact, however. Just ask them!

There are many ways that teachers and students can interact to show a mutual affection. One is to let the children talk about their problems and feelings. We, as adults, frequently seek people out to discuss problems we are having. Sometimes we seek advice, but often merely talking aloud about an issue allows us to get a different enough perspective to resolve the problem ourselves. Occasionally we become frustrated about something, and "blowing off steam" to someone permits us to put the frustration in a proper perspective. Talking also gives us a chance to follow an idea through from beginning to end, to spot weaknesses, and to formulate plans.

Children also benefit from discussing their problems. Guiding them to help find errors in their thinking is another means of helping them become more responsible for their activities. Allowing children to discuss issues that are important to them does not mean that we must become formal counselors to the children. The majority of teachers have not been trained to be counselors and, by acting in that capacity, they can do harm. Teachers can listen and determine whether children's problems are such that they should be referred to someone who does have counseling skills. Knowledge of when and how to refer is an important competency that all teachers should possess.

Behavior that is particularly offensive to a teacher can be discussed openly with the students. They can be urged to arrive at some type of resolution regarding that behavior. When children are involved in the decision-making process, they become personally involved and become much more accountable for their own behavior.

The need for cooperation can also be openly discussed with students. Sometimes we teachers come to school not feeling well. Rather than yelling or punishing the children for behavior that makes us feel even worse, we can deal with the problem directly by telling the children that we don't feel well and hope that they'll try particularly hard to keep the noise level down. It's surprising how well children can act when they are appealed to in a quiet, rational manner. Used sparingly, direct appeal can be an extremely effective means for classroom control.

Direct appeal coupled with open discussion can help students become accountable for their own behavior. It also helps the children to see that problems can be solved through rational rather than through physical means. Since there is always more than one side to an issue, aiding the students in recognizing problems and the multifaceted effects of the decision-making process can do much to help them develop skills in this area.

Clear, Simple Directions

How many times have we stopped driving in order to ask for directions, followed them for the first step or two, and then had to stop again because we couldn't remember the last part of the directions given? We usually react more to the fact that we have to spend time stopping again than to the fact that we can't remember. Yet students who have been able to process only the first couple of steps when following our directions are often chastised when they ask that the directions be repeated, or when they carry out the first steps of the directions and then start looking at their neighbors to see what they are supposed to do next. In essence, we ask that the children in our classroom be able to perform better than we are able to do.

Clear, simple directions are essential if we want the children to be able to complete their assignments. We've already mentioned memory span and how important it is to give directions in a way in which the children are able to process them. Multistage directions should not be given in a classroom until it is certain that every child for whom the directions are intended is able to follow them.

Vocabulary should also be simple and within the understanding of all the children involved. A single word can throw the children off the track they are trying to follow. If that single word is essential to the understanding of a total direction, the children will be unable to proceed beyond the point at which the word appears. Or, the word may be so distracting that the total message is lost because of the lack of understanding of the one word. This behavior is particularly characteristic of slow learners and of children with learning disabilities. Distractibilities sometimes get them all involved with a small word that really has little significance, but because of their inability to put things in proper perspective and to pick out what is the most important matter before them, they respond to insignificant matters or may be unable to respond at all.

Alerting strategies should be used when you are going to give directions, or when you are going to say something that the children should really attend to. A lead-in sentence such as "I'd like you all to listen carefully to what I have to say," can alert the students to what you have to say. When using this technique, it is important that you use it only when what you have to say is really important. Too frequent use or use when the subject is not really important can quickly turn off the student, and in the future no attention will be paid to the lead-in statements.

Reinforcement

Reinforcement is a topic that has received a great deal of attention during the past several years. We all know how important it is to reward what is desired so that the same activity will be repeated. We have previously discussed praise and how it can function in a classroom to obtain the behavior that we desire. Praise can be combined with immediate feedback to become a powerful reinforcer. Immediate feedback is important to the work children are performing as well as to their behavior exhibited. Just as children may hesitate to give the same answer that appeared on a test that has not yet been corrected and returned, so the children are not sure of repeating behavior that has been exhibited before if they are not sure whether the behavior is tolerated or forbidden.

Assuming you have given the children the rules of the classroom and the expectations for their behavior, it is important immediately to reinforce the behavior that you desire and to appropriately deal with the infractions of those that don't adhere to the conduct expected. The children will be much more comfortable with the knowledge that the rules are enforced. The behavior in the classroom will reflect this.

A particular problem arises when one child does something in the classroom to another child. Often the child has committed the offense because of the attention it brings, even though that attention may be of a negative nature. Behaviors of this type can often be eliminated by not giving attention to the aggressor, but to the child who has been the target of the behavior. One has to be extremely careful when doing this, however, for we don't want all of the children who have been jostled or touched to come running with a complaint because they know they will receive attention. A short statement such as "That's too bad, let's get back to work" may be far more effective over the long run, because the child who has committed the offense has not received the attention desired and the children who were affected do not get more than passing attention. By not overdoing the use of this technique, it should be possible to eliminate a lot of pure attention-getting behavior.

Extra work is another technique that we should look at as far as reinforcement is concerned. Very often we "reward" the child who finishes an assignment quickly by assigning more of the same type of work. Although this may be rewarding to the child who loves to do that type of activity, assigning more of the same really acts as a punishment to the children who are not particularly interested in the activity. A far better reinforcement for the children who finish early is to let them engage in an activity of their choice. Doing more of the same type of activity can be one of the choices you give the children, but there should be others so that the children are rewarded for their work, not punished.

Classroom Climate

Each of us has a different way of dealing with students. We shouldn't try to be the same, for each of us should try to be as effective as possible working in the way that we are most comfortable in working. Some of us are very informal and some of us are not. Some of us are very relaxed when dealing with students, while others of us are much more rigid. As we've said before, the type of personality that we have is not as important as is our consistency in the ways in which we work with students. Our basic personalities should not be changed unless they are such that they prohibit the children from learning. We can change certain things about our teaching, however, within the framework of the types of people that we are.

Have you ever thought about the type of classroom you run? Some of us would say that we run a "tight ship," while others might say that they "play it by ear." This is not the type of thing we are discussing, for those of us who run a "tight ship" as well as those of us who "play it by ear" can have the same type of climate within the classroom. By climate we refer to the type of teacher-child relationship that is fostered within the learning situation. When a child misses a question, how do you respond? With ridicule? With a definite "No, that's not right"? With some type of prompt that will help the child to answer correctly? If you are having trouble controlling a particular child have you ever examined the means that you are using to control that child? If children are afraid to answer questions because they may not have the right answer, have you ever thought the problem through as to the part you play in it?

By having an unbiased observer come into our rooms to help us determine the type of classroom climate that we have during our teaching sessions, we can help to answer many of the questions just asked. By having them administer a classroom observational instrument such as the Flanders, we can have a more objective means of looking at what we are doing in the classroom. The Flanders observational technique allows us to determine whether we are being positive and praising the children or negatively responding to them. A short observation period will allow us to know whether we are strictly a question-and-answer teacher or whether we try to get the children involved in discovering their own answers.

Instruments such as the Flanders allow us to look at our own teaching and try to improve it. By administering some type of observation instrument, our supervisors, principals, peers, or even parents can help us to examine objectively our teaching. If this type of aid from such people is not to your liking, it is possible to have your teaching videotaped and then to examine objectively your own teaching techniques.

The type of person who does your observation is not as important as the fact that you are trying to look at your own techniques. Sometimes an outsider can quickly tell us that we never say anything positive to the children, that we only let them know when something is not right. Others can tell us that we are only choosing those children to respond who we know will give us the answer that we want. They can also tell us if we always talk to one side of the room, or if we are unable to be heard at the back of the room. Whether this is the first year we have taught or the thirtieth, periodically we need to look objectively at our teaching. Whether we do it ourselves or involve others in the activity is not important, whether or not we do it is.

The use of humor in establishing a classroom climate is extremely important. Sometimes the right use of humor can dissolve an explosive situation into a good laugh, after which everyone is ready to settle down and get back to work. A direct confrontation can sometimes be resolved by the judicious use of humor. Rather than having to resolve a situation by sending the student to the principal's office, the use of humor can help both you and the students save face and get back to work.

Humor can also help someone out of a very embarrassing situation. One incident involved a lanky, gawky high school student who was growing so fast that he never was quite sure where his body was in space. Walking into a classroom, he unintentionally knocked a bookend away from the books his teacher had on her desk. The books quickly slid off the desk and onto the floor. In his efforts to catch the books, he turned and, with his body, knocked over a nearby bookcase. Turning to catch that, he turned over a chair. The whole class was waiting while the teacher looked at the complete chaos that the student had created. Knowing that all of it was unintentional, she smiled and said, "Let me know when you're through." All of the students laughed while they, the teacher, and the culprit straightened up the room. Once everything was back in place, the lesson was begun and everyone settled down immediately. Humor should not be used at someone's expense, however. If it is, that person soon becomes a scapegoat for the rest of the students and the victim becomes a class buffoon or withdraws. Either situation prevents the child from the most effective learning.

ADAPTING FOR COMMUNICATION PROBLEMS

Teachers frequently feel very frustrated when trying to communicate with children who have some type of speech problem. How long should you wait for children who are having a very severe speech block to get out their words? How often can you ask a child to repeat something you don't understand? It is very difficult to give specific answers to these questions, because much will depend upon the children, upon you, and upon the other students in the classroom.

The easiest way to understand children's speech is to learn what type of substitutions, omissions, additions, and distortions they are making. If you know that certain children always omit r's mentally substituting an r may help. This is very easy to do if there are only a few sounds that are affected. More often the children we are having difficulty understanding have many sounds that are affected, and so it is difficult mentally to carry out this type of activity.

You should feel free to ask the children several times to repeat their question or statement. After the children have repeated a couple of times and you are still unable to understand what has been said, you might ask the children to say it in another way. By doing that, the children may use words that are more comprehensible. (This is also a technique you can use if deaf children don't understand what you are saying.) You can ask the children to repeat the new way again, and if still unable to understand, you might ask the children's closest friends in the room to interpret for you. Anyone who communicates frequently with the children may learn the particular idiosyncrasies and be able to aid you. If this fails, ask the children to demonstrate with gestures or show you what is meant. You need to be very patient during this procedure and make it clear to the students that it is important that you understand what is being said.

One example of how you might use all of these methods and still not know what the child is trying to communicate comes to mind. A second-grade child used the sounds *uh-ee* to answer a question. Going through all of the mentioned techniques, the teacher had all of the reading group involved in trying to determine what was being said, for the boy had a very severe speech problem and rarely said anything either at school or at home. When the other children failed to aid, and the child shook his head indicating that he didn't know how to show what he had said, the teacher responded, "Well, it must be something . . . ," and before she could finish her statement, the child beamed brightly. *Something* was the word he had been trying to communicate. Thus, you may not always be able to use rational ways to decipher what a child is trying to communicate. You may just have to be lucky.

It is important to let the children who have some type of rhythm disorder know that they have plenty of time to say what they desire to say. It is also important to teach the other children in the room that you will wait for the message and will tolerate no interruptions on their part. Do not ask the children to think before they begin, or to take a big breath. Such techniques are not the cure for the problem, and the children know it. You may get some tips from the speech therapist about cues you can give to the children to remind them to use the techniques that they have learned in speech class for greater fluency.

If the children have taken a great deal of time and still are unable to communicate, you may ask if it is all right to go on to someone else and then come back to them. By doing this, you have not denied the children the communication they desire, but have given them relief from their embarrassment. Calling on another child and then going back to the children may be enough to allow the children to communicate.

Children who have speech problems need time to practice the speech they have learned in therapy in the classroom setting. Instead of merely handing out art papers, you can have children with speech problems pass them down the aisles, using speech in the process. "Would you like one?" or "What color would you like?" can be the types of responses you might have children use who are working on their *l*'s. The speech therapist will be able to provide you with the current sounds and behaviors each of your children is working on.

Show and tell, book reports, and verbal responses can be worked on in the children's individual therapy classes and then presented in the classroom if the children are particularly reluctant to speak in front of the group. Your acceptance of their problems and praise for their attempts can do much to aid them and contribute toward their acceptance by their peers.

Part 2
Bibliography

Apgar, V. and Beck, J. *Is my baby all right?* New York: Pocket Books, 1974.

Barraga, N. *Visual handicaps and learning.* Belmont, Ca.: Wadsworth Publishing Company, 1976.

Calovini, G. (ed.). *Mainstreaming the visually impaired child.* Springfield, Ill.: Instructional Materials Center, Office of the Superintendent of Public Instruction, State of Illinois.

Corn, A., and Martinez, I. *When you have a visually handicapped child in your classroom: Suggestions for teachers.* New York: American Foundation for the Blind, 1977.

Data Pak. *Facts about epilepsy and the many groups concerned with its medical and social management.* Washington, D.C. Epilepsy Foundation of America, n. d.

Davis, J. *Our forgotten children: Hard-of-hearing pupils in the schools.* Minneapolis: University of Minnesota, Audio-Visual Library Service, 1977.

Davis, H., and Silverman, R. *Hearing and deafness.* New York: Holt, Rinehart and Winston, 1978.

Flanders, N. *Analyzing teaching behavior.* Menlo Park, Ca.: Addison-Wesley Publishing Company, 1970.

Grotsky, J. (ed.). *The visually impaired and multi-handicapped.* Blackwood, N. J.: Potential Publishing Company, 1977.

Johnson, S., and Morasky, R. *Learning disabilities.* Boston: Allyn & Bacon, 1977.

Lilly, M. S. *Children with exceptional needs.* New York: Holt, Rinehart and Winston, 1979.

98

Lowenfeld, B. *The visually handicapped child in school.* New York: John Day, 1973.

Lowenfeld, B., Abel, G., and Hatlen, P. *Children learn to read.* Springfield, Ill.: Charles C Thomas, 1969.

Napier, G., Kappan, K., Tuttle, D., Schrotberger, W., and Dennison, A. *Handbook for teachers of the visually handicapped.* Louisville, Ky.: American Printing House for the Blind, 1974.

PART 3
PLANNING AND IMPLEMENTING THE EDUCATIONAL TASK

We have discussed the types of handicapped children who might be mainstreamed into the regular classroom and the ways that might be used to accommodate their handicaps. There is more to mainstreaming such children than accommodating to their handicaps, however. It is also necessary to adapt the tasks that they will be learning to their particular learning styles.

When we originally talked about looking at the children and the learning problems they presented, we talked about having to look at the children, the task they were learning, and the setting in which the task was being taught. Thus, the task itself is one very important part of the total process. We can adapt to the children very well, accepting the fact that they are unique individuals, but we will not be able to teach them in the most effective manner unless we also adapt the tasks they are to be taught. Presenting nothing but visual instruction to blind children or auditory instruction to the deaf children will not aid in teaching what must be taught. This section examines ways to look at the tasks themselves as well as means that have been used in the past for successfully working with handicapped children to enable them to function in the least restrictive environment.

CHAPTER 11
USE OF RECORDS AND ASSESSMENT INFORMATION

All children come to school with some type of records available to their teachers. Some material may be of minimal assistance in working academically with the children, such as immunization records. Others, such as records of achievement tests, past academic performance, and even attendance records, may be of considerable help. If children have poor word attack skills and also had a record of poor attendance while enrolled in their first-grade classes, chances are very strong that they may lack the information that was provided to the first graders on how to attack unfamiliar words. Thus, records can be extremely important in providing clues to children's problems.

Just as records can be extremely helpful, they can just as easily provide a bias against children who have had problems in schools. Reading previous teachers' comments on how uncooperative, belligerent, or how delayed children are may provide a mind set, thus perpetuating prior behaviors. Perhaps those previous behaviors were really a result of teachers taking a dislike to the children and failing to provide the type of environment in which the children could succeed.

In the past, if a question, often not directly pertaining to academic work, came up among a group of teachers in the teachers' lounge, anyone could go to the office and pull any child's folder. Since some records contained sordid tales, it was not unusual for several people to have knowledge of the content of particular children's folders. Early biases were promulgated and perpetuated. Innocent children became victims of malicious gossip about promiscuous mothers and abusive fathers.

The children's records also contained the results of various types of tests that had been given to them. Included may have been tests that were unfair to the children because they were standardized on a different population. Often a single test, one that was unfair to the children tested, was used to evaluate the children's learning potential. No consideration was given to

102

children who didn't feel well the day the tests were given. Many children had major decisions made about their future education on the basis of that one test. Many who used English as a second language were given low scores because they lacked an adequate command of the language and were subsequently assigned to classes for mentally retarded children. The same thing happened to children who had no contact with many of the middle-class experiences called for by some of the intelligence tests. Children didn't know answers because they had never heard some of the words used in the questions; nonetheless, they were sometimes labeled as retarded or disturbed and placed in special classes for their entire school careers. Thus, test results failed to show functioning levels or potentials, but instead showed how able children were to give answers demanded by the test manual of a particular test.

Sometimes students who were placed in special classes in this way were kept in these classes because they were never retested to give evidence of a higher level of functioning. Some states demanded the enrollment of a certain number of similarly labeled children in order for a class to be eligible for state money to reimburse the local school district for the cost of the classroom. Occasionally school district personnel would deliberately not retest a child who had been discriminated against in initial testing and who later turned out to be normal in intelligence because there would not be sufficient numbers to meet the state enrollment figures if the child were retested and returned to the regular class. Rather then having the local district assume the cost of the program, the child was kept in the class.

Because of factors similar to this, many children were denied their basic rights. The authors of P.L. 94–142 were aware of such policies, and so the right to due process was built into the law. Children are now protected from misclassification, mislabeling, and from the denial of equal education. Before it can be determined that any child should be assigned special education, that child must be given a formal assessment. Such assessment is to be nondiscriminating. P.L. 94–142 states that handicapped children are to be evaluated with more than one test, examined only with instruments appropriate to them, and that such instruments must have been developed and standardized on children similar to those children being tested. It also states that children are to be tested in their native language.

ASSESSMENT

From the time they enter school, children are given all types of assessments. Through the years, quite a bit of information may be added to their folders. The folders of children who have been identified as handicapped will contain the results of psychological tests that were administered to help determine their level of functioning when they were first identified. Updates may be included. Otological, audiological, opthalmological, occupational and physical therapy, and dental information may also be included. Reports of former teachers, as well as results of any attainment tests that a particular school system requires, will also be contained. Folders may also include teacher-made tests, checklists of attainments, attitude scales, anecdotal records, observations, interviews, case studies, and samples of past work.

Children who are currently being assessed as to whether special education services are needed will also have folders. These folders will contain many of the same types of evaluation measures. To determine whether the children should be assigned special education, the content and appropriateness of such evaluative measures, both formal and informal, need to be assessed.

Formal tests may consist of several types. One is the individual intelligence test that is administered by the school psychologist or psychometrician. The psychologist administers the most appropriate test to the children, taking into consideration the protection against discriminative testing that is part of P.L. 94–142. Individualized intelligence tests are *norm-referenced tests*. A norm-referenced test is given to a number of children so that a standard response can be obtained from children similar in age, background, experience, and so on. Some tests have statistics to show that they have adequate standardization. Others do not. The American Psychological Association has set up guidelines that should be followed in standardizing or norming a test. Such guidelines stipulate that the standardization group should follow the same profile as the country's population according to the latest U. S. census regarding sex, urban, rural, race, socioeconomic conditions, and so forth. By being standardized on such a group, the chances of the test unfairly discriminating becomes much less. To ask city children to name the part of a cow that produces milk—when the children might think that the corner grocer produces it—is just as discriminatory as asking rural children questions about the urban transportation system. Thus, it becomes important to give the type of test that will allow the children the greatest advantage in the test situation. As a teacher, you should make sure that norm-referenced tests are used appropriately for the children being assessed.

Other types of norm-referenced tests will assess academic achievement, language, perceptual, adaptive, social-cultural, emotional, and environmental behaviors. Children should never be assessed on the basis of only one test, for there is no single test available that gives enough information for the children's future to be determined on the basis of that one test. Norm-referenced tests give us a particular type of information that is not available with other types of tests. They tell us how children compare with others of the same age and grade. Thus, we get a general idea of what the children are lacking to be able to perform at the same level as others, supposedly similar to themselves.

The types of achievement tests that are used in most school systems are norm-referenced. They have been standardized on a large population of children with particular characteristics. Thus, the children from your class

who are given the same instrument are being compared to the norms obtained from that standardization group. Norm-referenced test results cover a
range of scores, and the scores your children obtain are compared to that
range. The children may receive a grade level of functioning, a percentile
score, or a ranking. Children may be said to be functioning at a percentile
point when compared with the norm group. One child may be at the fiftieth
percentile of all second graders in the norm-referenced group, another may
be at the ninetieth percentile, and another at the twentieth percentile.
Others may be said to be functioning at the first-grade level, the sixth-grade
level, or the second-grade level. This should be interpreted to mean that
compared with all second graders, one is functioning below, at first grade
level. Compared with all second graders on which the test was standardized,
one was functioning enough higher to be considered at a sixth-grade level,
and one was on a second-grade level, or at the average of the standardization
group. Still others will be ranked according to where they stand within a
standardized group of 100 children, one at 18, another at 64, and another at
96. Again, they are compared with the results of the group that was used for
the standardization procedures.

Norm-referenced tests are used to document the achievement levels of
children within a classroom or system. They can be used to show progress
over time and can help identify weaknesses in teaching particular subject
matter. Administrators use them for such purposes when determining subject matter content and textbooks or to document the efficacy of particular
programs. They also use them to compare performances in different schools
within the system, to compare individual children with their peers, and for
research data. When considering the scores from such tests, it should be
determined whether the children being tested are similar to the children on
whom the tests were standardized and whether the reliability of the tests is
documented at .80 or higher. If not, the scores earned should be suspect, and
little credibility given them.

Tests are usually mandated by school boards to make sure that the
children within their particular school systems continue to learn. Sometimes
teacher contracts are dependent upon students obtaining certain scores
when compared to the norms.

It is true that norm-referenced tests can give us a general idea of how
children are functioning when compared with the test standardization
groups, but they may be of little help in identifying where particular children are having learning difficulties. They may provide little information
that can be used directly in our teaching or specific assessment for special
education purposes.

The results of formally administered norm-referenced achievement
tests will give a general idea of level of functioning. A score of grade two will
tell you that the child is functioning at the second-grade level as compared
with the standardization group. However, three children who test at that
second-grade level may be functioning in very different ways. One may

have three subtests of grade one, grade two, and grade three. Another may have subtests of grade two, grade two, and grade two. The third may have subtests of grade zero, grade two, and grade four. However, all of the children will average out at the second-grade level. Obviously, we must have additional information if we wish to find out where our children are having problems, particularly if we wish to find the answers to those problems quickly and efficiently.

Norm-referenced tests do not give us specific information as to the particular types of problems that children may be having in a particular subject. They may tell us that the children are having problems in, say, reading comprehension, but they usually cannot tell us what specific problems the children are having with such comprehension. To do that, we usually go to informal tests. Criterion-referenced tests are usually used for this purpose.

Criterion-referenced tests have not been normed on a large population of children. Instead, the teacher has chosen a particular criterion and has compared how the children are doing regarding that particular criterion. Suppose the teacher has set up reciting the alphabet as the particular objective. She or he compares each child's functioning against that criterion: John knows all the letters up to l; Susie knows all of the vowels; Jimmy gets l, m, n, o, and p mixed up; and Doreen knows them all. By evaluating the children in this manner, the teacher will have a much better idea of where to start with the children as far as setting particular teaching objectives is concerned. To find where all of the children are functioning in all of their subjects, it will be necessary to construct several criterion-referenced tests. It will also be necessary to administer more than one in each of the subject areas taught.

Criterion-referenced tests set up an end goal for the children. Criteria are specified as to what the children must do to meet that objective or goal. Thus, the children are evaluated as to how they function in terms of an absolute or specific criterion. The test does not consider how the children react in relationship to their peers.

Just as the norm-referenced tests have shortcomings in that the children may not be similar to the norming population, so criterion-referenced tests can be discriminatory. What if the criterion chosen is inappropriate to the needs of the children? What should be done if the children have not learned a particular designated task? By considering the strengths and weaknesses of each of the tests administered, and there should be many of them, a profile can be formed regarding the children who are being evaluated. However, when looking at the instruments that have been used, the question of reliability and validity should be carefully examined.

Reliability refers to whether or not the test is consistent. Will the children get the same score if the test is readministered? To know how consistent a test is, a standard error of measurement is included with standardized test information. The standard error tells how much that test score may vary on a test-retest basis. Tests that have a large standard error are not as useful as those that have a small number. A large discrepancy in scores on a test-retest basis may result in children seeming to require special education on one day and not on another. This may be a factor of the lack of reliability of the test, not a deficiency of the children. To be nondiscriminatory, such factors should be taken into consideration.

Another factor to consider is that of validity. Does the instrument test what it purports to test? We have all taken little quizzes that have been part of magazine or newspaper articles and wondered when we were through what the particular items included had to do with the subject at hand. We must be especially careful of test validity in testing children. If children perform poorly on a geography test, was it because the children were poor readers and could not adequately follow the directions or did the children not know the subject of geography? A good test will not allow one reason to be mistaken for the other. A good teacher will also be able to differentiate between one and the other. But a single test will not be sufficient; several examples of the children's ability will be necessary to determine the reason.

OBSERVATION

In determining children's ability, information in addition to that already mentioned will be necessary. Previous records are often helpful. Interviews with those who have worked with the children previously can often be of a great assistance in determining problems. This is why referring teachers are a necessary part of the evaluation team.

Observation of the children in a variety of settings will also be of help. Observations can consist of several types. Informal observation in the natural setting can help to get a general idea of the children. The school psychologist or social worker may come into the classroom to observe particular children. A naturalistic observation usually gives an overall picture of the setting and how the children function within that setting. A description of the children is usually a part of it, and any interaction between the children and the environment during the observation is duly written down as part of the observation:

> During the spelling class Jack was noted to be reading a comic book which was carefully masked with his spelling book. He held the spelling book half open with the cover facing the teacher.

This could also be written:

> During spelling class, Jack kept sneaking looks at a comic book.

In the first report we know what Jack was doing and how he was achieving it, while in the second we react to the word *sneak*. Personal biases must be kept out of these observations, for reporting them in prejudicial terms may effect the outcome for the children, resulting in inappropriate plans.

There are both formal and informal observation systems that can be used when observing children. Some systems are used to determine the climate of the classroom that we have discussed previously. A psychologist may do a formal evaluation of the class in which a child is presently enrolled. By observing the teacher and the responses between the teacher and the children in the class it is possible to determine whether that teacher is a critical person, authoritarian, reinforcing, and so on. Sometimes children with certain personality characteristics have difficulty functioning in a classroom where a teacher is very intolerant of such characteristics. Merely placing a child with a different teacher may eliminate the problems.

Some norm-referenced observation techniques are available which examine the interaction between a specific child and the teacher or between a specific child and other children in the classroom. Such interaction can be part of the total picture: Is the child consistent in behavior? Does that child react to adults differently than to peers? How do the other children react to the child? This should be written, not in subjective terms, such as "The other children don't like John," but in terms such as "When John neared a small group of three boys, they turned their backs on him. One boy told him to 'Go play somewhere else.' "

Observation can also be on a very informal basis. A daily log might be such an informal means of keeping track of behavior. It is important, however, not to let subjective feelings color the way in which the child is perceived. Facts are important to substantiate the observation.

Baseline data is another type of information that can be obtained from observations. The type of information that needs to be obtained will determine what type of data you collect. Let's say that John is seldom in his seat. In fact, you believe that increasing his in-seat behavior would do much to help his other problems—he bothers the other children while they are working, he doesn't finish his work, he's not paying attention while he wanders around the room and then doesn't know what to do when he finally does take his seat, and so forth. You might want to keep track of several bits of data at the same time to verify all of this.

To take information relevant to the situation, you would have to determine whether you want to keep track of numbers of incidences, duration of time, or whether or not the behavior occurred. To do this, your incidences must be observable and measurable. If you decide to use the number of incidences to measure John's leaving his seat, you may not get very helpful information. The child may have only one time recorded—he may leave his seat just one time but be out of it for the entire morning! Thus, the number of incidences may not be helpful. It might be helpful, however, to record the number of minutes that John was in his seat. You could record the total number of minutes the child is in his seat and compare the numbers as you continue to record your data. A change in number will tell you the in-seat behavior is increasing or decreasing. On the other hand, you may merely want to know if John left his seat during the time that seatwork was assigned. A + or − could be assigned during the time period sampled. An increase or decrease in the numbers of times sampled would tell whether the behavior is increasing or decreasing. Thus, the appropriate type of data to be gathered becomes important. Observation data can be extremely helpful, but these data must be both valid and reliable to be of use.

Other types of observations can be used to help determine where children are having particular difficulties, and these will be discussed later. Observation, however, is a key in helping to meet the needs of individual children. Finding the problems and helping to solve them demand that teachers play the roles of good detectives, and observation is a key part in that role. Observations that are factual in nature can help in great measure to meet the children's needs.

THE ASSESSMENT TEAM

The first time you have a handicapped child assigned to your room, the assessment team will have already met and decided that the most appropriate setting for the child is in your classroom. The information from the assessment team will be included in the development of an individualized education plan (i.e.p.) for the child. The i.e.p. will have been produced by those who have had the child before, and it will accompany the child so that you as the receiving teacher will know the long- and short-term goals that have been designated as needed for that particular child to develop to the highest degree of ability.

Public Law 94–142 specifies that an i.e.p. shall be developed for all handicapped children receiving any type of special education services. This plan is to be developed after the children have been deemed in need of special educational services by an interdisciplinary assessment. The assessment is to take into consideration the children's particular handicapping conditions and is to be free of cultural biases. The evaluation team membership will vary according to each child's needs, but educational and psychological reports are necessary. It is the teacher who verifies that the children have particular problems with learning, and the psychologist who administers restricted tests to the children. Medical personnel, physical therapists, occupational therapists, speech therapists, social workers, and others may be a part of different teams, with the composition varying for each child evaluated.

The teacher who has worked with the children should be able to give specific examples of the types of learning problems and behaviors exhibited by them. In time you will have to play that role, and so we will discuss it. The teacher who has dealt with the children and who knows the particular problems is the most logical person to help with the assessment.

Formal and informal tests, records, observations, and interviews, then, should all be part of the data upon which the children's needs are determined. After each team member has assessed the children and the information is gathered, the assessment team will meet to discuss its findings. When you become part of this team, it is important for you to speak up and include everything you think relevant to the case and to argue for the children if you disagree with the findings of others. The reason this is so necessary is that the ultimate responsibility for implementing the program that is proposed for the children will rest with you as the teacher. If you disagree with the findings and fail to speak out, you will be responsible for implementing a program with which you disagree.

Many teachers are intimidated when they face a multidisciplinary team and are afraid to speak out in contradiction to the findings of "experts." You shouldn't be. Teachers are the ones who deal with the children on a regular basis. You are the "expert" as far as the educational setting is concerned. The other team members may have examined the children individually for a very limited period of time, but they do not have the wealth of information that you as a teacher have gathered over a longer period. Children may react very differently in a one-to-one situation than in a group setting. It is important that other team members know how the children function in several settings. It is also important that you present this information in a factual, unbiased manner and as briefly as possible. Many disciplinary team members may have been turned off in the past by teachers who rambled on in generalities without data to substantiate their claims. Accurate information from the tests and observations may do much to inform the other team members and may also aid them in their future dealings with other teachers.

It is important that the team deal with the total child, strengths as well as weaknesses. The more informed the team can be about the children, the better the recommendations will be. Your voice may be the only one of advocacy for some children, and those children depend upon you to represent them well. Since the ultimate responsibility for implementation will be yours, it is important that you assume some of the responsibility for getting accurate and realistic recommendations from the team members. The more help you get from the team, the easier your job will be. If the information they are contributing is incomplete or not helpful, speak up. The team members won't know unless you tell them.

CONFIDENTIALITY AND ACCESSIBILITY

If a good job is carried out by those gathering information regarding the children, there should be considerable information in their folders. So that this information will not be misused, P.L. 94–142 stipulates the confidentiality and accessibility regarding them. Every school system must have a procedure regarding these factors. Folders are to be kept in a monitored area and to be available only to those directly involved with the children. The school system must establish who is to have access to the records and the manner in which this information will be kept so that confidentiality and accessibility will be assured. No longer will teachers be allowed to look at any child's folder. Teachers also must exhibit much greater care when adding information to the folders. Objective data is necessary and subjective data no longer has a place when it might prejudice the reader against the children. Such protection will prevent the type of information that was seen in the past when a mother may have been reported as attending a conference in a drunken state when in fact she was suffering from a balance problem. Or when a middle-class teacher reacted to persons of the lower class who could not afford the type of clothing that the teacher felt necessary. It means that teachers will have to be responsible and accountable for the information that they write into the records. It means that unfounded statements will no longer be included. We must stick to facts.

The children's parents and the children, if appropriate, are guaranteed access to the folder. If the parents disagree with some of the information and want something deleted, they have the right to make that request. Even facts can be used to prejudice teachers against children. A child who is listed as blind and the cause of blindness recorded as congenital syphilis may still be the victim of prejudice. One mother asked that the cause of her child's blindness be deleted from the record because she felt that it affected her relationship with the teachers.

If members of the team feel that the information requested to be removed is vital to the children and should not be removed, parents have the right to put into writing why they wanted it removed and that written statement has to be inserted into the record. If the parents wish to press the case for removal even further, they can ask for a hearing regarding the matter. The hearing, conducted as a legal matter, will determine the relative merits and determine whether the material will be included or deleted.

Keeping accurate and factual records will do much to aid us as teachers in our search for information regarding our children's learning problems. All information found in the children's records can aid us in helping them if such information is accurate and relevant.

INDIVIDUALIZED EDUCATION PROGRAMS (i.e.p.)

After determining as much as possible regarding the children's particular learning problems through a complete appraisal, the assessment team makes the recommendation for appropriate placement based upon a consideration of all the material included. The parents must be notified and approve of this placement. Once the parents' approval of the placement has been determined, an individual education plan (i.e.p.) must be formed to meet the needs of the children. A team gets together to write the children's i.e.p. According to P.L. 94–142, that team must have a minimal membership. The membership will consist of a representative of the local school district responsible for the children's education, the children's teachers, and the children's parents. A district representative must be present even though the children may currently be in some type of private facility, because the responsibility for the children's education, according to P.L. 94–142, lies with the local school district. The district representative, the children's teacher, the children's parent(s), and others relevant to the needs of the particular children will be part of the i.e.p. team. The determination of those whose presence is apropos is determined during the assessment team conference during which specific members identify particular services needed by the children. You, as the children's teacher, will become involved the next time the i.e.p. conference is held if you weren't the original time.

The goal of the i.e.p. conference is to establish long- and short-term objectives that are appropriate to the needs of each of the particular children. These objectives, required by law, are to provide some type of accountability to the plan developed for the children. Many children in the past were kept in settings entirely inappropriate to their needs, and so this is an attempt to design a program needed by the children and then to see that appropriate programming is implemented.

The i.e.p. conference has been dreaded by many teachers because of the need to work with other disciplines and with parents. This dread is unfortunate, for such conferences can bring out relevant contributions by the local district representatives as well as by the parents. The i.e.p. team must have open communication between its members. Any vocabulary that you do not understand, you should ask to be defined. The use of terms specific to each discipline is the number one factor that team members feel interferes with true communication. It is necessary, then, to have the team members specify what they mean. In time, you may learn these terms because of frequent contact with them. You must make sure that all team members, especially the parents, understand them before you use them however.

Teachers who have not written an i.e.p. are often anxious about the format and length needed. There is no uniform i.e.p. form that can be provided here that will meet each school district's requirements. Some states provide a precise format. Other states provide a general format which each district adapts to its own needs. The length of individual i.e.p.s may vary from a few sentences to many pages. Thus, the format will depend upon your state, your district, your team, the children being planned for, and, specifically, upon you. Since you, as the teacher, will be the one implementing most of the i.e.p., your needs for specificity will have to be met.

P.L. 94–142 does stipulate the essentials that are to be found in the i.e.p. There must be included a statement of the child's present levels of educational performance; the annual goals, including short-term instructional objectives; the specific special education and related services to be provided to the child and the extent to which the child will be able to participate in the regular educational program; the projected dates for the initiation of services and the anticipated duration of the services; and the appropriate objective criteria and evaluation procedures and schedules for determining, on at least an annual basis, whether the short-term instructional objectives are being achieved. These essentials must be included. The format and length in which they are presented will vary.

Although the length changes, the definitiveness should not. Goals should be measurable, should have the criteria for that measurement, and should define the approximate date when they should be met. To say that John Smith will "learn addition facts" is not enough. You need to know that John Smith will "learn addition facts, in various combinations from 1 to 5, by March 15 to 90 percent criteria." This gives you a definite objective to work towards. It also allows you to make realistic short-term goals, for the ability to add figures 4 and 5 doesn't occur the same week as determining the one-to-one correspondence between an object and a number.

The i.e.p., then, is the plan from which you will work. It helps you to remain on target. It also allows you to act as the children's advocate in seeing that other services are provided. You are not expected to provide everything the children need. If the i.e.p. specifies special education resource room assistance, the children should have it. If "speech twice a week for a half hour period," is specified, the children should be receiving it. That's what the i.e.p. is all about, to meet the needs of each child.

The i.e.p. should begin by including the present level of functioning as well as the goals that you want to meet. The present level of functioning is determined from the assessment information found in the children's records. By beginning with the present level of functioning, you can make sure that the goals written are realistic. This prevents you and other team members from wishful thinking. Sometimes we want very much for the children to attain more than is objectively possible. Or we may be fatalistic and think the children can't learn. Including the present level of functioning keeps us realistically focused.

Long-term goals are established once it is determined at which level the children are functioning. These goals are determined by the children's past rate of progression as you consider at what level they should be functioning at the end of the current school year. There should be long-term goals encompassing each of the subject areas in your curriculum. The goals have to be written in behavioral terms, and they must be measurable and observable with levels of competency determined. Thus, we cannot say that "for the year our goal is for John to become a good citizen," because we have no criteria for measuring good citizenship in children. However, we could say that by the end of the term we want John to know six primary duties of the mayor and city council with 100 percent accuracy. Since research has shown that children learn more rapidly if we break a task down into smaller parts than if we teach the terminal or whole task, we would break the long-term objective into smaller, shorter ones. The first short-term objective that we might teach as part of this long-term objective might be to identify and list the primary duties of the mayor.

Specific long- and short-term goals must be established for each curriculum area. All goals must be agreed to by all members sitting on the i.e.p.

team, and each must affix his or her signature attesting that they accept the educational plan. After the i.e.p. conference, you as the teacher, will take the short-term goals and develop an education plan. This is accomplished by breaking down the short-term goal into teachable tasks, or lesson plans. This involves some type of task analysis. However, before the teachable tasks are determined, it is necessary to know if John has the prerequisite skills for such tasks. Does John know what a mayor is and have a general idea of how the mayor might function? If John doesn't, the short-term task needs to be rewritten into more elementary steps and these prerequisites included.

CHAPTER 12
TEACHING THE TASK

Earlier we said that we must be good detectives in order to determine the causes of the problems that children exhibit when in our classrooms. Sometimes the problems lie in the children and sometimes in a handicapping condition, in prior experiences, or in behavior. At other times it may lie in the task we are trying to teach. Perhaps we haven't presented the task in a manner in which the children can learn.

We probably all have had situations arise when things have been presented in a manner in which we cannot learn. The command of a college professor to "Don't write this down, just listen and you'll understand," when we can never remember anything given in that manner, is an example. Complicated directions given when we can't find a specific location may be meaningless, and we may have to stop again to get them straight. The "handful of this" and a "pinch of that" may be sufficient for some cooks but disastrous for others.

We all have specific strengths and weaknesses and learn best when the task is presented so that we are able to learn it. It sometimes takes an excellent detective to find out specifically what the best presentation is. One college student was having a particularly difficult time learning to hear differences in sounds. Since she was preparing to teach speech to deaf students, it was extremely important for her to be able to do this. She studied her textbooks carefully, read all the supplementary readings as well, and still was unable to distinguish the differences between a "good" and a "poor" sound production. The auditory modality was tried, and she went through several taped sequences of carefully programmed sound production tapes. She spent hours trying to learn. Special sessions were devised for her. Tutors tore their hair over her lack of progress. Finally, deciding to look at her own problems as she had been taught to look at others, she discovered why she had been unable to learn by means of these methods—she was a tactile learner! She found it necessary to trace the shape of the sounds in the air and on paper. She held her hand against her face as she produced the various sounds. She carefully felt her tongue, teeth, and lip movements as she produced the sounds. By going back over the visual and auditory material and adding this tactual element, she quickly learned the material. In a very short time she had progressed to the level of the rest of the class when even her fellow students had been ready to give up on her such a short time before.

When looking at problems of learning residing within the child, within the task we have presented, or within a particular setting in which we are presenting the task, the former example illustrates something that was discovered regarding the child, in this case a college student, who learned only by incorporating the tactual modality. The presentation of the material in a tactile modality, however, was a part of the task. Thus, something found within the child may necessitate a change in our task presentation. If a child is totally blind, we might present information in the auditory modality. If the child were profoundly deaf, that modality could not be used, but we might try the visual modality supplemented by tactual input. Presentation must be made so that our students can learn the material presented. Thus, not only must various aspects of what the child brings to the task be looked at, the task must also be examined. The techniques that we have for examining the tasks can provide us with information regarding why a child is not learning, if we are good detectives and know how to look.

PREREQUISITE SKILLS

Before we begin to analyze the task, we must ask the question of whether or not the task is an appropriate one for the children to learn. We've already discussed the functioning level of the student. General functioning level may not give us enough information regarding specific prerequisite skills, however, and we must be sure that the children have the prerequisite skills to learn a task. If the children are unable to add, subtract, and multiply, we would say that they do not have the prerequisite skills necessary to learn division, because they would be unable to carry out the division process without the use of these prerequisite skills. If the children are unable to do a specific division problem, though, we would not be able to identify, without further investigation, which of the areas—addition, subtraction, or multiplication—was the prerequisite skill missing. By careful assessment, we might discover one area responsible or there might be serious deficiencies in each of them.

Most of our prerequisite skill identification is not so easy as observing problems with addition, subtraction, or multiplication, and we must think things through in identifying prerequisite skills as we choose appropriate tasks for our children to learn. Sometimes we may have to teach some of the prerequisite skills before we can go on and teach the task that we have identified. For example, when we look at spelling prerequisites, there are many. In order for the child to spell words correctly, there must not only be the prerequisites for spelling but for holding a pencil, for forming the letters, and for putting these letters on paper. To these must be added the ability to spell both phonetic as well as nonphonetic words with word attack skills for those that are unfamiliar. The children must be able to discriminate various sounds and their spellings. For some words there must be knowledge of rules for spelling, as well as for adding prefixes and suffixes to roots. The children must also be able to identify syllables as they occur in speech and be able to reproduce them in writing. Otherwise spelling becomes a rote skill in which words are learned for a test on Friday and quickly forgotten by Monday.

If we plan so that our children learn carefully sequenced behavior, and keep accurate data regarding the children's progress, we will be able to identify whether they have prerequisite skills. By having specific knowledge of the information previously learned, we can be assured that the children are ready for subsequent skills. The children have a decided advantage in learning the task when they are ready for the introduction of such a task. If they do not have the prerequisite skills, we are almost assuredly planning them for failure.

Looking at the errors children make can allow us to verify whether these prerequisites are present. By examining spelling errors, we would look to see if the children have reversed the consonants, vowels, or syllables. Is there a phonetic spelling of a nonphonetic word? Is there a wrong association of a sound with a particular letter? Is there a relationship between the letters written and the thought the children were trying to communicate? Do the children omit or add letters to those needed? Do they mispronounce words and spell the words in the same manner that they speak them? Do they combine any two or more of the errors listed?

By specifically examining the errors, then, we can obtain information as to whether or not children have prerequisite skills for a specific task to be taught. Although it is preferred that the children's records contain the specificity with which they have learned previous material, they may not. If not, it will be necessary for you to initiate a task to verify whether there is adequate knowledge of prerequisite skills.

ERROR ANALYSIS

Let us take some particular examples of task analysis in arithmetic, reading and spelling to see if we can identify the tasks to be taught and the prerequisite skills needed by doing a type of error analysis.

Errors in Arithmetic

If we use $6)\overline{2767}$ as a problem, we can begin to get some idea of the difficulty the children are having. If a particular child has responded to the problem in the following way, we can examine the results for possible errors.

$$\begin{array}{r} 409 \\ 6\overline{)2767} \\ \underline{24} \\ 067 \\ \underline{63} \\ 4 \end{array}$$

We can see that the child has the basic idea of division as far as the first step is concerned. The child has supposedly determined that the 6 goes into the 27 four times and has placed the 4 and the 24 in the proper places. At this point, there is a question of what the child did and why. The 24 is not subtracted from the 27. We don't know why, however. Does the child know the number is to be subtracted? Why is there a 0 placed under the 4? Is it possible that we gave the children an example of division in which we put a zero under the numbers, and the child has generalized this 0 as a step to be taken each time? Right now we don't know the answer. All we know is that there is a 0 there.

The child next places a 6 next to the 0. This is a correct procedure. However, the child also placed a 7 next to the 06. Why? We don't know. Did the child bring both numbers down at once? If only the 0 and 6 were there, they could have been divided by the 6 in the divisor one time, and the 1 would go in the answer. Instead, there is a 0 there. Why? Again, we don't know. The child seems to have used the 067 and divided it by 9. The number subtracted is 63, and we don't know where that number came from either. Six times 9 is 54, not 63. Does the child know all the multiplication facts?

One way we can find out where the children are having difficulty is to have them work the problem out loud, explaining what they are doing and why they are doing it. As the children perform the task, we can monitor them to see where the errors are being made. Since we can't have the children perform our task aloud in this instance, we have to make some type of tentative judgment by merely looking at the problem as it was completed.

If children make errors in arithmetic, the errors are usually of four types: The children copied the problem incorrectly; the children made errors in the basic number combinations of addition, subtraction, multiplication, or division; the children were unable to carry out basic math applications; or there was an error or lack of knowledge regarding the operational procedures to be used in a particular instance.

If we look at these four possibilities here, we can tell that the child was able to copy the problem correctly. The numbers are lined up correctly, and this does not seem to be the problem. There is a question of whether or not the child has the basic number facts down correctly. The 0 presents a problem. Does the child know the number facts when 0 is used? Does the child know the multiplication tables using 6s? Does the child know the number combinations when 4 is taken away from 7? There is also a question of whether or not the child was able to carry out the basic math application. Did the child know that the 24 was to be subtracted from the 27? The 63 was subtracted from the 67, why not the 24 from the 27? There also appears to be a problem in the operational procedures to be used. Two numbers were brought down at the same time from the dividend. Did the child do this in one step or two? Does the child know what is to be done with the remainder?

We cannot tell the answers to our questions by merely looking at the one problem. These questions can lead us to the answers, however. We can give the child simple problems that can help us pinpoint the exact source of the problems. We can have the child demonstrate whether the 0 and 6 multiplication processes are the source of the difficulty by having that child perform some multiplication problems. We can have the child perform some basic one-number divisor problems to see if the child knows how to bring down numbers from the dividend. If the child is able to do that, we can present some problems in which one number in the divisor is used but the dividend will have double numbers. We can also use a number in the dividend where the child will not be able to divide the divisor into it and the use of a 0 will be necessary. By having the child perform tasks in all of these areas, we can then look for consistency in the errors. Sometimes an error will be mere carelessness, and subsequent problems will not elicit the same type of errors. However, if there is a real difficulty with some part of the task that is required, consistency will be seen at that step where the child is having difficulty.

Let's look at the same problem performed by another child. The $6\overline{)2767}$ is worked in the following manner:

Figure 12.1.

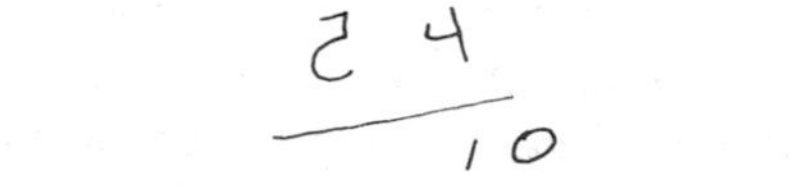

In the first place, the child has miscopied the problem. Both 7s were copied as 4s and the 2 as a 3. Does the child know the difference? We can see that the child seems to know some of the basic facts involved, although there is some question about 6 × 1. There also seems to be problems with alignment of the numbers used, a lack of knowledge of basic subtraction application, and the operational procedures to be used. The child has left a remainder larger than the divisor. There is also a consistency in the reversal of the number 5.

The same procedure needs to be carried out as with the last student. Some informal testing needs to be carried out to see if the errors are consistent and whether the child has the prerequisite skills to answer the problems. The prerequisite skills in this case are all of the skills we have talked about: the ability to copy the problem correctly, the multiplication tables involving 6s, subtraction facts, and the operational procedures to carry out dividing with a one-number divisor.

If the children lack the prerequisite skills, we will have to teach those skills. Only by identifying what skills are needed can we be sure whether or not the children possess such skills. With an error analysis we can determine whether the child has committed such errors as applying the appropriate steps but out of sequence, skipping steps, or applying the wrong tactic for a needed operation.

In the error analysis used for the last problem, we noted that the child consistently reversed the number 5 when writing it. When analyzing these skills of writing, it is important to know whether any reversals used are a result of motor problems involving the motor ability to carry out the task or whether there is a problem having to do with the process involved in writing. If the child is motorically unable to carry out the task, then we go into the handicap a child is presenting rather than the task itself, and we may need to think of adaptations such as a typewriter with a template so that the child can control fine motor-hand movements enough to type out the letters needed. If the lack of motor development is normal for the age of the child, we may need to wait to introduce an activity until the child has the prerequisite skills necessary, assuming that the skill we wish to teach is age appropriate.

We don't worry too much about reversals until a child is over nine years of age. Up to that time reversals are very common and are not considered a problem for unusual concern. Since children ordinarily don't establish a dominant hand for writing until they are seven years of age or older, we don't worry about writing reversals until the children are more than nine years of age. We point out the errors so the children will learn to recognize them, but we don't give inordinate attention.

Errors in Reading and Spelling

The way children read can give us many cues to the manner in which we need to present reading tasks. Some children are poor readers because they have had poor reading teachers during the critical early years of beginning reading. They will have reading problems, but those problems are not qualitatively different from normal children. Children who have a true dyslexia are different in qualitative as well as quantitative measures. While children with specific reading disorders have the potential for normal reading, they are usually one to two years below the normal reading levels. Children with a true dyslexic condition may be considerably below those levels. Children with a true dyslexia will usually be found in a special education setting, for intensive work is needed to deal with this very serious learning disability.

Some children who have reading problems have a problem making out the visual configuration of the words. There is a poor memory for the visual gestalt. They may be able to read by sounding out the words very carefully. The children who have this type of problem may be able to read a word list at or very near to their grade level but do it by very laboriously sounding out each letter. The children have difficulty remembering what particular letters look like. Children who have reached the fourth or fifth grade may still be having difficulty remembering how the various letters are formed. Children with this type of reading problem are able to take very unfamiliar words and read them phonetically, but familiar words that are spelled nonphonetically will stump them. Because of this problem, a difficult word such as *apparatus* might be able to be read while a familiar word such as *laugh* might present problems.

The difficulties with spelling parallel those of reading. The children with this type of learning problem are able to spell phonetically but may not be able to spell words that are nonphonetically spelled. The spelling of such words may be poor but not bizarre. As a teacher, you will be able to make out what the child has spelled by phonetically reading what has been spelled. Vacation will be spelled phonetically as "vakashun." Although it is not correct, the children who spell in this manner can get their messages across.

Other children will be able to read only by sight. They read by gestalt, with no word attack skills. These children will get a visual configuration and will read the words accordingly. Because they have to remember the whole word and have no word attack skills, the unknown words present problems to them. There is also the difficulty that after a certain number of words are learned, other words begin to have the same type of visual configuration. Thus, *apparatus* and *opposites* may look very similar in configuration, and if the children have no ability to sound out letters or to know the sounds the letters might make, they cannot distinguish between the two words. By the time children with this type of learning problem reach the fourth or fifth grades, they are already limited in their reading vocabularies. Although the initial sight reading vocabularies that are taught to beginning readers may make these children appear to have no difficulties, later, as the need for word attack skills is manifested, these children run into serious difficulties.

These children also have great discrepancies in their spelling ability. Words that are known and familiar are spelled correctly. Words that are completely nonphonetic may be spelled correctly, while words that are unknown will be spelled incorrectly, even though they may be very short and simple words. Because there are no word attack skills, the children may choose a similar visual configuration and substitute that word for the desired word. The word substituted may be totally inappropriate, but the children will be unaware of the difference. Words that are known and that the children are able to spell may be substituted for unknown words. Thus, the word *funny* may be substituted either for the read or written word *laugh*.

A few children have severe reading problems that will not be overcome unless given considerable help and remediation. These children have a combination of the two types of problems discussed above, and they are not able visually to remember the configuration of a word or to spell out that word phonetically. These children have no sight vocabulary and no word attack skills. They are unable to learn the configuration of letters. They may learn a few words from the primer or preprimer readers, but those words have usually been conditioned in and the children are not able to generalize them.

The spelling of these children is bizarre because of the lack of visual and auditory skills. The children confuse the letters, reverse them, and are unable to differentiate those with subtle differences such as *b* and *p*. It is these children who need the special help of special educators who have the skills to remediate their problems. Without specific help, these children will end their education as illiterate students.

Work Examples

Let us now examine examples of work that may be submitted by the above types of students so that we can do an error analysis to see what prerequisite skills they are missing and the type of tasks we should present to them.

Figure 12.2.

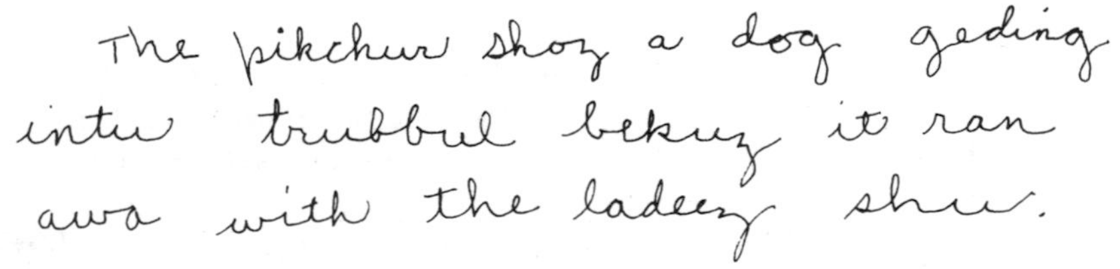

The pikchur shoz a dog geding intu trubbul bekuz it ran awa with the ladeez shu.

As can be seen, it is possible to read this sentence through and to make out what the child wished to communicate if one reads the words phonetically. Although many of the words are spelled wrong, they are spelled as they sound. This is the type of child who needs help in recognizing that all letters are not read or spelled as they sound. The child needs the prerequisite skills of attacking nonphonetically spelled words. For this purpose, we may use the Phonovisual materials and teach the child various spellings for the same sound. The Open Court Series may be used because of its multisensory approach. Or we may use the Northamption (Yale) Chart (see figure 12.3) to attain the same purpose. Each of these techniques uses an approach that helps the children learn that sounds can be spelled in different ways. Thus, the long e sound ($\bar{e}$) can be spelled, and look like, ee, e, ea, or e-e. We must go through the steps that we originally used to teach the

Figure 12.3. Northampton (Yale) Chart

CONSONANT SOUNDS

```
h—
wh      w—
p       b       m
t       d       n       l       r
k       g̓       ng
ck
c
f       v
ph
th¹     th²
s¹      z
c(e)    s²
c(i)
c(y)
sh      zh      y—
ch      j               x = ks        qu = kwh
tch     g²
        g—
        —ge
        dge
```

VOWEL SOUNDS

```
oo¹     oo²     o—e     aw            —o—
(r) u–e         oa      au
(r) ew          —o²     o(r)
                ow

ee      —i—     a–e     —e—           —a—
 –e     —y      ai      ea²
 ea¹            ay
 e–e

        a(r)    —u—     ur
                —a      er
                        ir

a—e     i–e     o–e     ou      oi    u–e
ai      igh     oa      ow¹     oy    ew
ay      –y      —o²
                ow
```

123

phonics of letters and teach the child that there are other spellings that can sound the same as the letters that have already been learned.

In the Northampton (Yale) Chart, the primary or most usual spellings are displayed as the larger letters. Other spellings that are used for the same sounds are given in smaller print, with the most usual secondary spelling listed just below the primary spelling and the tertiary spelling below that. These spellings can help the child who has a very phonetic approach to reading and spelling to learn to spell such words as *teacher*, which uses primary, secondary, and tertiary spellings.

By using the chart, children who have only a phonetic approach to words can use their strength, analyzing phonetically, to read more sight words. By learning that letters have more than one sound, they can use the new secondary and tertiary spellings to sound out words. By using these strengths, they will gradually increase their visual modality to discriminate the shape of the words and the letters used within the words. By carefully programming the task that has been analyzed, the child should eventually be able to apply these spellings to words. By carefully analyzing their errors and teaching the missing prerequisite skills, both reading and spelling should improve considerably. The task varies considerably, however, when analyzing the errors of a child who has only a sight vocabulary to attack words.

Figure 12.4.

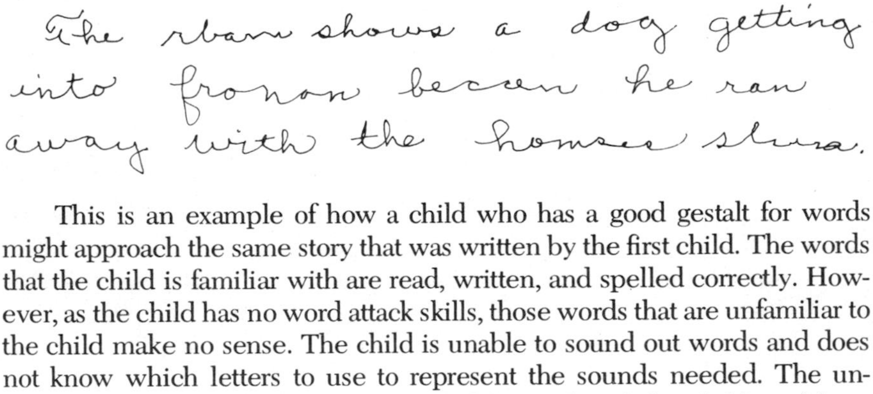

This is an example of how a child who has a good gestalt for words might approach the same story that was written by the first child. The words that the child is familiar with are read, written, and spelled correctly. However, as the child has no word attack skills, those words that are unfamiliar to the child make no sense. The child is unable to sound out words and does not know which letters to use to represent the sounds needed. The unknown words, then, are read or spelled bizarrely. If the child is able to remember part of the word, such as in the word *because*, the part remembered will have the correct visual formation, but beyond the point at which the child forgets the gestalt the word will make no sense, visually or auditorally. Only those words that the child can revisualize will be read or spelled correctly.

Teaching reading mechanics is necessary before teaching reading comprehension—it will be necessary to train the child in the sounds of the letters. Since the child has been unable to learn the sounds of letters, it will be necessary to teach the sounds through new means so that the child can obtain new ways to approach words that are unfamiliar. This may mean tracing the letters as they are heard and sounded out. Sandpaper letters, writing in clay, and writing in the air are all techniques that have proven effective. Once the primary spellings of sounds are learned, these children should also be exposed to secondary and tertiary spellings. Visual-auditory-tactile and kinesthetic modalities need to be included when learning these spellings also. The child who presents the greatest difficulty is the third child, the one who has neither a phonetic nor a visual approach to reading.

Figure 12.5.

This is typical of the type of response that this child will give in an attempt to write a story. The child will be unable to read, other than for an occasional word such as the *the* used to start the story. Spelling will also be bizarre. An error analysis results in the listing of many missing prerequisite skills. Spelling errors usually result because a child is unable to visualize the word, relies too much on auditory cues, or doesn't know spelling rules. In this case, all three areas have deficiencies. In essence, this child is a nonreader as well as a nonspeller. Such children will have to begin at the very beginning to learn to read. They will need a multisensory approach and considerable time in order to learn to read by this method. Children with this type of problem will usually withdraw from tasks involving reading and may show a decided sense of inferiority regarding school activities. These children may act out or demonstrate other types of abnormal behaviors in an attempt to draw attention away from their inadequacies.

The types of error analysis we have done may not give us exact answers to the problems we are seeking to solve. They will enable us to know how to test further to specify the particular problem that a child is having. Thus, we can determine if prerequisite skills need to be taught. Once this is accomplished, it is necessary to analyze the task to be learned.

TASK ANALYSIS

There is really no right or wrong way to do a task analysis as far as the number of steps and the procedures to use. You may start with the final step and go backwards to find each step that is needed to complete the task. Or, you may start at the beginning and go through the whole sequence.

Let's take the simple task of toothbrushing to illustrate how we might approach analyzing a task. We'll use this because it's a motor task that differs greatly among people. Since you brush your teeth each day, you should be fairly able to analyze the task, right? Write down the steps that you go through in your toothbrushing routine.

Your task may look something like this:

Get toothpaste and toothbrush.
Take off toothpaste cap and put paste on brush.
Brush teeth.
Rinse mouth.
Put paste and brush away.

Or, it may look something like this:

Child locates sink.
Child locates toothpaste.
Child grasps toothpaste and holds.
Child removes cap from toothpaste.
Child sets cap on edge of sink.
Child locates brush.
Child grasps brush and places on edge of sink.
Child uses both hands to squeeze paste onto brush.
Child takes cap from edge of sink and replaces on paste.
Child replaces toothpaste tube to original location.
Child picks up toothbrush with paste on it.
Child raises brush to mouth.
Child opens mouth.
Child places brush on teeth and moves brush back and forth.
Etc.

It cannot be said that either of these two methods is incorrect as far as a task analysis is concerned. Neither may be correct as far as a particular child is concerned. One may have too much in one step in the sequence and the other may not have enough. The appropriateness of the task analysis will depend upon the needs of the children involved. You know from introducing new material to the children in your classroom that some children will get the material no matter how grossly you present it. Present a mere idea of what is required, and some children take the idea and run with it. The majority of the children will require more information, and so you usually gear your instruction to that level. You break it down a little more than you would for those who grasp ideas quickly.

There always seems to be one or two children that don't grasp the idea from your group presentation. Those are the children that need to have the task analyzed even further. You may not know which of the children will need this further breakdown of tasks until you have tried to teach the task and the children don't all grasp the concept you are trying to teach. At this point, you look at the work of the children and try to find the errors of those children who have not yet gotten the concept to see where it is that they have strayed from the task as you were trying to teach it. It is at this point that you break the task down into finer and finer component skills, thus allowing the children to identify the subskills that must be learned in order for the complete task to be conquered.

It may be necessary for you to analyze the task a bit differently for different children. The idea of error analysis thus becomes an important concept in teaching children. We begin to look at what is supposed to be performed versus what the children are actually doing. We can then identify what behavior the children are lacking but that they need in order to begin learning the new task. It is from such an examination that we obtain the instructional sequence that we want the children to achieve.

Let's go back to the toothbrushing task again. Is it better to wet the brush before or after the toothpaste is added? Or is it necessary to wet the brush at all? Let's say that the child to whom we are teaching the task is blind. If that child wets the brush after the paste is added, there is the chance that the toothpaste will be washed away. Since there is no particular reason for wetting the brush, unless one is using tooth powder, the task becomes much simpler if the step of wetting the brush is eliminated and the child applies the toothpaste directly to the dry toothbrush and then continues to brush the teeth without dampening the brush.

It is important to remember that the simplest way becomes the most efficient way in teaching children. Do not add extra steps unless it makes the task easier for the children to learn. Sometimes by adding steps we confuse the children and make it more difficult rather than easier for them.

Sometimes we have to adapt steps because the children are unable physically to perform certain steps in the sequence. A child who is crippled and has no wrist rotation may not be able to screw the cap off the toothpaste. Or a child may lack the strength to squeeze the toothpaste from the tube. In this case, it may be necessary to have some type of adaptive equipment to squeeze the paste from the tube, or it may be necessary for some sort of alternative to be used, such as toothpowder, the cap of which can be easily removed with the lips and no squeezing is necessary to obtain the contents. However, in this case, it is necessary to dampen the brush for the toothpowder to adhere to the brush. Thus, we must weigh the total programming in the task to make sure that our adaptation will not take more effort than the original step that we were trying to eliminate.

We can learn much by looking at the task the children are trying to perform. If we look at the type of errors, we can get an idea of how we need to change the task so that the children can learn it. If the children are consistent in the types of errors they make, we begin to see where the task breaks down.

Thus, our first step is to identify the prerequisite skills that the children need in order to perform the task. Another is to determine the type of learning that we want the children to do. Do we merely want the children to have an acquaintance with the subject or do we want them to know the task in detail and be able to apply it in a variety of settings? Are we expecting too much from children who are just beginning to acquire knowledge of a task? Are we reviewing a task the children have already attained or are we teaching a brand new task? The stage of acquisition is important in determining the task and how it is taught.

STAGES OF LEARNING ACQUISITION

The stages of acquisition that we'll talk about here are initial acquisition, proficiency, maintenance, and generalization. Each stage is approached differently as far as task analysis is concerned. Initial acquisition is the stage at which the children are first exposed to the task and are beginning to get the idea of how the task is to be done. Since the information is new, it is necessary to present it in an organized, logical manner. Simple vocabulary as well as both visual and verbal input should be used. At this stage, a careful watch of where the children are and how the task needs to be modified is necessary. The frustration level at this stage is usually low. Teachers need to be very alert to the types of difficulties the children are experiencing. If a good job is done at this stage, as far as teaching is concerned, the other stages usually follow uneventfully. To aid this in happening, each child needs to be observed carefully, and any errors made should be carefully analyzed to see where it is that the child is floundering.

Once the children have the idea of what is being taught and have the skills necessary for initial acquisition, it is necessary for those children to build proficiency in that task. Merely learning to read a few words is not enough to be proficient in the task of reading. We must have many opportunities to use the skills we have learned or they are quickly forgotten. Only by applying the skills over and over do the children become proficient. Those children who have many opportunities to read quickly learn their skills and are able to use the skills with greater and greater proficiency.

Once the children become proficient, it is important to maintain the skills that have been learned. Do you remember how to derive a square root? Chances are you only remember if you have had to use it frequently. Those who teach it will remember it because they have maintained their skills. Those who have not had to use it lose their proficiency with it and have to go through the whole process again in order to refresh their memories. And so it is with the children we teach. Once we have taught a skill, it is important to keep giving the children opportunities to use the information so that they can maintain the skills in which they have formerly become proficient. Otherwise, the skills are quickly lost. Once the children become truly proficient in a task they should be able to work independently and without errors. Once they are able to do this, periodic opportunities should be provided for them to practice these skills so they don't forget them. This is the maintenance level.

It is also important to give the children opportunities to generalize the information. If the children are only exposed to information within the confines of a textbook, it allows few opportunities for them to generalize their skills to the real world. The children may be able to learn the facts written in an arithmetic textbook and see no relevancy to the real world. The children may learn their simple facts, become proficient in them, and maintain them over time without seeing that they can be used to see what size package is more economical when grocery shopping for their mothers. Children may learn number facts and not know how to generalize their use to figure out how many chairs they must get when another third grade comes into their room to view a presentation. It becomes important, then, to not only teach to the proficiency and maintenance stages, but also to allow the children the opportunities to generalize what they have learned to other situations within the school as well as outside the school in true-to-life settings.

In analyzing the task and setting it up to teach the children, we as teachers must be very aware of what we are doing. To insure that the children experience success while they are learning what we are teaching, we must be aware of what we are teaching. Not only must we be aware of whether the child is in the initial acquisition, proficiency, maintenance, or generalization stages, but we must program appropriately for these stages.

If the child is in the initial acquisition stage, there should only be one type of response required on each page of problems given. If we are teaching subtraction and this is the initial phase, there should be nothing added to the page to confuse the children. Later we can determine whether or not the children can differentiate between addition and subtraction, but we don't want to confuse the issue at the initial stage. Otherwise we won't know if the errors are because the children don't understand subtraction or if they don't understand addition. During the proficiency and maintenance stages we must also carefully determine whether the practice we are giving the students is teaching proficiency and maintenance or if we are introducing something new into the material that will confuse the students, and us, as we look to see where the students are experiencing difficulty. We must also decide how we can aid the children as they encounter problems and help them learn the material. What verbal and visual cues and prompts can we give the children to aid them in mastery? How can we fade these cues and prompts to help the children along in their attainment? Children may need help at any particular point in this analysis. We should be ready to provide the assistance they need.

Thus, after we have analyzed the task and through teaching have established the point at which we need to further break down the task, we can aid the children in meeting the criterion measures that we have set. We should have prepared our initial objectives based upon what we knew about the children and then have begun an instructional sequence that would help the children reach those objectives. Once we begin to implement a task, we can continue to examine the task, looking at the errors to tell us where the children are still having difficulty. We should then test to see if the children have initial acquisition, proficiency, maintenance, and generalization. We must revise and go through the whole sequence again if the task remains unlearned.

CHAPTER 13
CLASSROOM ADAPTATIONS

Many of the techniques you are currently using will be appropriate when planning and implementing educational tasks for handicapped children. You may need to adapt certain others for specific children. If you are not using the following techniques in your classroom, you may want to consider how you can incorporate them into your present style and methodology, for they have proven effective in the past not only with children who have particular educational problems but with all kinds of children.

SCHEDULES

Children who have a need for structure can get a great deal of support from a specific routine. Therefore, it pays to have a definite schedule in the classroom. Oftentimes students who are unable to schedule themselves and get bogged down in one activity and are unable to go on to the next, can accomplish much by using a schedule that the teacher has developed. Children who have limited attention spans, who perseverate in their activities, and who have difficulty transferring from one activity to another, can all benefit from a carefully developed schedule.

Several considerations should be made in developing the schedule. The most important or difficult subjects should be undertaken while the students are fresh. This is the reason why reading is usually taught the first thing in the morning during the first few grades in school. It is an important subject, and since it underlies most other academic subjects, it is essential that the students have a firm foundation in it. Thus, the children with educational problems are not different from their peers. Consideration should be given to when the children are the most alert and to the specific subjects they are having difficulty with.

It is important that the students have a schedule that is consistent so

130

they can rely on it. Changes in that schedule should not be made until the children are familiar with the schedule and then are carefully prepared for changes. It is necessary to alter our schedules occasionally. School plays, parties, parent conferences, and early dismissals can all necessitate changes. It is vital that our students be prepared ahead of time for such changes. Mentioning it the day before, again the first thing in the morning, and periodically throughout the day will result in less disturbance when the actual schedule change is made.

After the children have become familiar with a schedule and are comfortable with it, we need to begin deliberately to alter that schedule. We want the students to become flexible and also to become more able to structure things themselves. Thus, after the students have become accustomed to the schedule, deliberate changes can be made, with less and less preparation given the students ahead of time. If carefully programmed, the students can become more and more able to schedule themselves and less and less upset by changes in routine.

CHANGING ACTIVITIES

Many children have considerable difficulty changing from one activity to another. Some of us are very hesitant when we are asked to change activities quickly. A call to dinner may be ignored until we finish the page we are reading. Or we may respond, "In a minute," or "I'll be there as soon as I finish this." We don't give children in the classroom the same opportunity to finish their work, however. We just ask them to put away one activity and to begin another. This may be very upsetting to some children.

One way we can help these students to change activities is to give warnings to the children a few minutes before the change is to take place. Five minutes before an activity is to cease, children can be warned that they should finish their work, because they will have to put it away in five minutes. You may repeat the warning in two minutes. Then, when the time is up, instructions are given to put the work away. The children will have been prepared for this and are usually much more able to make the change without difficulty. Timers can also be used for warning purposes if we set them a few minutes before a task is to end. Timers are often very effective because they are inanimate objects. Children may react negatively to us when we remind them, but rarely do they react to a timer. Individual timers may be set for specific children, according to their needs. As the children get used to changing activities, accepting the warnings, and better able to judge time, a single warning a couple of minutes before the change of activities is desired will be enough. The children will then be able to make an uneventful transition.

It is important when announcing the change in activities to use only one command at a time. "Put away your work," is sometimes all that a particular student can process. "Get out your reading books" is another.

Then add, "Turn to page 32." If we initially say, "Put away your work, get out your reading books, and turn to page 32," as a three-stage command, children may not respond, not because they are unable to do these activities, but because they are unable to follow a three-stage command. Until we have verified that every child in the classroom is able to follow three-stage commands, we should not use them in the classroom.

GROUPING THE CHILDREN

With all the things that have been mentioned about individualizing instruction, it's very easy at this stage to wonder how you'll find time to carry out all of the activities needed for the special children who have been mainstreamed into your classroom and at the same time be able to do justice to all the other students in your class. Although the thought of it all can be a little overwhelming, there is a way that it can be managed. Even though you'll want to individualize instruction for all of the children, grouping is a logical way to handle numbers of children. You can still individualize, even though you group the children. It won't be the type of grouping that is used with the "bluebirds," "redbirds," and "yellowbirds," but it is grouping, and it will allow you to find the number of hours in the day to meet all of the children's objectives.

The former type of grouping, in which the teacher initially places each child into one of three or so groups and then gives the group a name, is a much more static way of dealing with students. It very often results in rather inflexible groups, and there is not much mobility among them. It assumes that the children are similar in learning ability, rate, and style in all of the material that will be covered during the reading task. In practice, however, the individual students learn different objectives at different rates and in different ways. Keeping them within the same group means that they must progress in the same manner as the majority of group members. A more adaptable method is needed if we are to individualize truly.

When thinking of how to group the children, it is best to list the short-term objectives that have been determined through your evaluation procedures. Look at the short-term objectives and decide whether there are similarities among them. It is from these objectives that you form your groups of children. Group size will vary from objective to objective, but that is not a major consideration because the groups will not be static in membership throughout the year. As soon as one objective is met, the new short-term objectives will be examined for new group membership. Because the needs of individual children are not identical, the membership will change from objective to objective. This will allow the children to be grouped with different peers throughout the school year and will avoid the stigma of the children knowing that they are in the "dumb group." Some groups may last a few days while other may last months, depending on the objectives.

The easiest way to keep track of the groupings is to make a master chart of the skills your children need. Choose one skill where the children are functioning at a similar level and task analyze it to meet the needs of most of the children. It is important to remember that some of the children may have to be put in a separate group later on because they will need the task further analyzed in order to learn it. However, the majority of the children will be able to meet the objective in the way in which you first task analyze it if you do a thorough job.

The steps in the task analysis can then be written along the left-hand side of a sheet of paper. Heavy construction paper or tag board is good for this purpose, particularly if you think that the task to be learned will take some time. The chart will become your record of attainment as well as your list of objectives and grouping, so durability is desired for tasks that may take a little time.

After the task has been analyzed and the steps written down the left-hand side of the paper, the students' names should be written across the top of the page. Make a graph by drawing lines the length and width of the page between each step. Your graph will look like that in figure 13.1. Notice that all of the spaces following 1 digit + 1 digit, no regrouping, have been filled in. That is to show that all of the children have the prerequisite skill— solving addition facts with sums up to 18. The outline of the space under each name is to signify that each child is now working on that skill. The child is not yet competent in the skill, but is working on it. As you work with the group, the squares will be filled in to the degree that each child has reached: initial acquisition, proficiency, maintenance, and generalization. Initial acquisition will be marked with the date the child initially acquired the skill. Proficiency is noted by the filling in of the top half of the square. Maintenance is noted by filling in the bottom part of the square, and generalization by writing the date in a different color over the square. After a few weeks of work, the chart will look like that in figure 13.2. As you can see, the groups are working on the same objective but are not all at the same spot. As is true in most cases, the majority of the group will remain together, but there will be a couple of children that will need more time and will have to have the task broken down into further steps.

Once the objectives have been reached, the group is disbanded, and if the long-range objective is to be continued, the total group will again be looked at to see where all of the children are in their short-term objectives. New groups will be formed. If Dawn, Chris, and Ian continue to learn at a slower rate than the rest of their group, it may be that they will be in a different group with other children. By keeping track of all of the children in this manner, it is possible to regroup continually to meet the needs of your children. They, in turn, will learn that you are very interested in them as

Figure 13.1.

	John	Joe	Sue	Jennifer	Dawn	Kevin	Chris	Scott	Ian
1 digit + 1 digit no regrouping									
2 digits + 1 digit no regrouping									
2 digits + 2 digits no regrouping									
3 digits + 1 digit no regrouping									
3 digits + 2 digits no regrouping									
3 digits + 3 digits no regrouping									

Figure 13.2.

	John	Joe	Sue	Jennifer	Dawn	Kevin	Chris	Scott	Ian
1 digit + 1 digit no regrouping									
2 digits + 1 digit no regrouping	10/3 11/4	10/10	10/11 11/5	9/30 11/14		10/11		10/1	
2 digits + 2 digits no regrouping									
3 digits + 1 digit no regrouping									
3 digits + 2 digits no regrouping									
3 digits + 3 digits no regrouping									

individuals, and the fact that they are placed in different groups during the year will avoid the negative connotations of grouping that have been a part of school children's lives in the past.

RECORDING BEHAVIOR

Even if you have no direct help teaching the children, others can often help you by recording the efforts of the children in your classroom. Some type of records need to be kept of the stages of learning so you can properly plan for

Figure 13.3.

10	10	10	10	10	10	10	10	10	10	10	10	10	10	10	10	10	10
9	9	9	9	9	9	9	9	9	9	9	9	9	9	9	9	9	9
8	8	8	8	8	8	8	8	8	8	8	8	8	8	8	8	8	8
7	7	7	7	7	7	7	7	7	7	7	7	7	7	7	7	7	7
6	6	6	6	6	6	6	6	6	6	6	6	6	6	6	6	6	6
5	5	5	5	5	5	5	5	5	5	5	5	5	5	5	5	5	5
4	4	4	4	4	4	4	4	4	4	4	4	4	4	4	4	4	4
3	3	3	3	3	3	3	3	3	3	3	3	3	3	3	3	3	3
2	2	2	2	2	2	2	2	2	2	2	2	2	2	2	2	2	2
1	1	1	1	1	1	1	1	1	1	1	1	1	1	1	1	1	1

the children. The figures shown depict probably the easiest and fastest means of recording that you can find. You may find others that better meet your specific needs and you should use them. Some school systems require that you use a particular system to record. The following is included for those of you who have not found a system that allows you to record quickly the various children in your class.

The basic system is shown in figure 13.3. If a child does something right, you circle the number. If the child fails that item, you draw a mark through the number. See figure 13.4. By looking at the last number with a line or a circle, you can tell the total number of times that the child was questioned or the total number of problems that the child was asked to complete.

By placing the dates and the activity above a particular column, you can keep a record of progress over time as shown in figure 13.5. By using a different color than you used to mark the number correct, or by using a different type of mark, you can graph the continuing progress of the child. The graph is formed by counting the number of problems that the child got right each day and making a mark around that number. The graph can also be used to determine what colors or letters the child is or isn't learning. By counting the number correct you can still graph the learning curve. See figures 13.6 and 13.7.

Figure 13.4.

~~10~~	~~10~~	(10)	~~10~~	~~10~~	10	10	10	10	10	10	10	10	10	10	10	10	10
~~9~~	~~9~~	~~9~~	~~9~~	~~9~~	9	9	9	9	9	9	9	9	9	9	9	9	9
~~8~~	~~8~~	~~8~~	~~8~~	~~8~~	8	8	8	8	8	8	8	8	8	8	8	8	8
~~7~~	~~7~~	~~7~~	~~7~~	(7)	7	7	7	7	7	7	7	7	7	7	7	7	7
~~6~~	(6)	~~6~~	~~6~~	~~6~~	6	6	6	6	6	6	6	6	6	6	6	6	6
~~5~~	~~5~~	~~5~~	(5)	~~5~~	5	5	5	5	5	5	5	5	5	5	5	5	5
~~4~~	~~4~~	~~4~~	(4)	(4)	4	4	4	4	4	4	4	4	4	4	4	4	4
~~3~~	(3)	(3)	(3)	~~3~~	3	3	3	3	3	3	3	3	3	3	3	3	3
~~2~~	~~2~~	~~2~~	~~2~~	(2)	2	2	2	2	2	2	2	2	2	2	2	2	2
(1)	(1)	(1)	~~1~~	(1)	1	1	1	1	1	1	1	1	1	1	1	1	1

Figure 13.5.

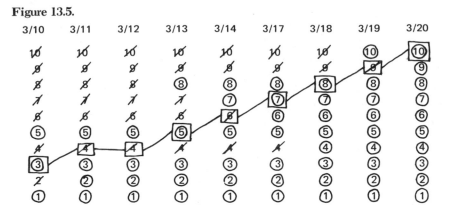

The charts show that the child is making a gradual improvement in the number of letters and colors. We can also pinpoint the exact point at which the child is having difficulty and teach to that difficulty.

We can also use the same type of chart in group activities. By heading the various columns with the different children's names, we can chart a whole group at one time. If you later desire, you can cut the columns apart and paste each child's graph to a separate page. You can thus chart a group's progress but still have a record of each separate child's individual growth. There are many activities for which the children will be able to chart their own growth. This will take less of your time and give the children incentive as they see their growth charts improve.

Records can also be kept in this manner of the undesired behaviors of the children and of antecedent and consequential behaviors by having those behaviors head the columns. If the same antecedent behavior is noted before each behavior, and you note the same consequence that followed, it gives reason to investigage the relationship and to come up with new methods for dealing with it.

Recording can help us in many ways. Very often we think that behavior is improving, and it may be, but we might be ignoring other behaviors that are taking place. One such instance comes to mind in which a child's ear-

Figure 13.6.

9	red	red	red	red	red	red	red	red
8	yellow	yellow	yellow	yellow	yellow	yellow	yellow	yellow
7	blue	blue	blue	blue	blue	blue	blue	blue
6	orange	orange	orange	orange	orange	orange	orange	orange
5	green	green	green	green	green	green	green	green
4	purple	purple	purple	purple	purple	purple	purple	purple
3	brown	brown	brown	brown	brown	brown	brown	brown
2	black	black	black	black	black	black	black	black
1	white	white	white	white	white	white	white	white

Figure 13.7.

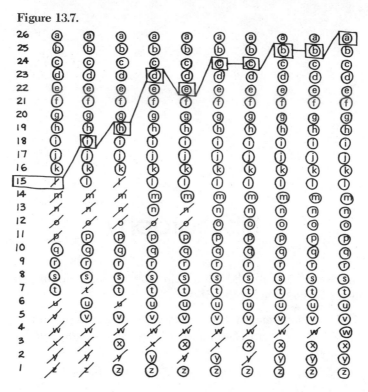

slapping behavior was programmed for extinction. A very good learning curve showed that the behavior was, indeed, diminishing. At the same time, however, another chart of abnormal behavior showed that the child was beginning to bite others in direct proportion to the decrease in ear slapping. When the biting behavior was targeted, the charts showed that behavior well under control, but at the same time a pinching behavior was increasing in indirect ratio to the decrease in biting. If there were no charts or records of the behaviors, we could well have patted ourselves on the back and told everyone about our success. By keeping records we recognized that teaching a behavior that would use both hands constructively could aid in eliminating the use of hands in abnormal behavior.

Behavior is not a single entity that can be looked at and treated without looking at the total child, the type of handicap, and the way that handicap has been treated in the past, the type of task that is being presented to the child, and the setting in which the task is to be learned or performed. Only by considering each can we plan constructively. Only by examining each will we be able to solve the problem of "something's wrong but I'm not sure what." By careful consideration of all three elements, we can see real growth taking place. By considering all three, as a classroom teacher who has taken on the responsibility of educating an exceptional learner, we will see the child bloom and blossom in the least restrictive environment.

Part 3
Bibliography

American Foundation for the Blind. *Catalog of publications.* New York: American Foundation for the Blind.

Boder, E. Developmental dyslexia: A diagnostic approach on three atypical reading-spelling patterns. *Developmental Medicine and Child Neurology,* 1973, 15, 663.

Flanders, N. *Analyzing teaching behavior.* Menlo Park, Ca.: Addison-Wesley Publishing Company, 1970.

Lowenbraun, S., and Affleck, J. *Teaching mildly handicapped children in regular classes.* Columbus, Oh.: Charles Merrill Publishing Company, 1976.

Moran, M. *Assessment of the exceptional learner in the regular classroom.* Denver: Love Publishing Company, 1978.

Northampton Charts. Adapted from Yale, C. Formation, and development of English Elementary Sounds, found in H. Davis and R. Silverman, *Hearing and deafness.* New York: Holt, Rinehart and Winston, 1970.

Open Court Basic Readers. LaSalle, Ill.: Open Court Publishing Co., 1965.

P.L. 94–142, *Federal Register.* Tuesday, August 23, 1977.

Wallace, G., and Larsen, S. *Educational assessment of learning problems: Testing for teaching.* Boston: Allyn & Bacon, 1978.

Wiederholt, J. L., Hammill, D., and Brown, V. *The resource teacher: A guide to effective practices.* Boston: Allyn & Bacon, 1978.

PART 4
PLANNING THE EDUCATIONAL SETTING

In discussing the search for the solutions of problems that our children present, we have talked about the difficulties that the children might bring to us as a result of their handicapping conditions, the impact of those conditions, the ways that we might examine and present the tasks that we want to teach them, and how we look at the settings in which we teach the children these tasks. The setting in which you are attempting to have the child perform the task may be responsible for the child being unable to complete it, rather than an inability to perform the task itself. For example, one preschooler who was very physically handicapped was being encouraged to feed himself his lunch. Placed alongside the other children on one side of the lunch table, he never seemed able to complete this task. Looking for the possible reason, the child's handicapping physical condition was considered. Although cerebral palsy prevented normal use of his hands and arms, he was able to get them to his mouth. The handicapping condition didn't seem to be the problem; he moved very slowly, but the total time consumed was well within the normal lunch period allowed.

It was decided to look at the task itself. The task of self-feeding had been carefully broken down into steps that the child had been able to attain. During the initial teaching there were several steps that had to be further analyzed, but he was now able to go through the complete sequence, with some adaptations allowed for his physical problems, and could complete the eating and drinking sequence necessary for eating independently.

Since the problem seemed to lie in neither the child nor the task, the setting was carefully examined. Indeed, the answer seemed to lie in this area. Seated alongside the other children, this child seemed too distracted by the others to pay attention to his food. Although he had the skills necessary to feed himself, he was not paying enough attention to the task to

139

complete it in the allowed time. Therefore, a change in setting seemed indicated.

The child was placed at a small table in another part of the room, with his back to the rest of the children. Unfortunately, the location was considered only as it related to the rest of the children. Subsequently, it was noticed that the table faced an area where the child was able to see out a glass door that faced a very busy intersection. The distraction of the other children was forgotten and in its place came a preoccupation with the events taking place at the intersection outside the door. Clearly, this setting was as distracting as the first.

The setting was then changed to one that had been constructed for distractible learning disabled children. The sections of the blackboards in the room could swing out to form carrels for the children. Two blackboard sections were pulled open and the child placed in the resulting small space. There were no distracting influences on the sections of the board or on the wall that the child faced. This setting did not meet the child's needs, however, as he turned and stretched to observe the children who were grouped at the table in another part of the room. In fact, his desire to view the other children was so great that his balance was often threatened by his twisting and turning. A screen to further eliminate distractions proved equally ineffective.

Another setting was tried and that proved to be effective. The child was placed in a position where he could view all of the other children while eating at the same time. His classmates were placed along the outsides of two tables that were placed in the shape of the V. The child himself was seated at the base of the V so he was able to observe all of the children without having to move his head. Although he was placed in a setting that had more people in it than in the prior three settings, this proved to be the most effective, and the child was able to finish his meals within the allotted time.

Many problems with settings are not as easily solved. It takes considerable time to seek out the specific difficulty, but if the problem is not found to be with the child or with the task that you have as an objective, the resolution must be with the setting. Although an examination of the setting is important to all children in that it affects their ability to function, it is particularly important as it relates to handicapped children, for they have fewer coping skills. All of us may be disturbed when someone around us whistles or talks as we try to concentrate, but we are usually able to continue our activities as they continue their annoyances. Many disabled children are unable to do this, however. The distractions are too great. Thus, the setting becomes particularly important to their functioning.

CHAPTER 14
STRUCTURING THE CLASSROOM

If you as a teacher ask for help in dealing with a particular child, the person you have sought out to give this help will be unable to deal effectively with the many ramifications of the problems unless the actual classroom is observed at a time when your behaviors as well as those of the child and the child's classmates are typical of the behaviors that have resulted in your concerns. All the individuals involved must be observed within the classroom environment. For effective observations, specific objectives for the observations must be set. Basically, we want to observe the child, the group that the child is in, and your interactions with the child and the others in the group. It is necessary to observe the settings in which the problems occur and the events that occur just prior to the behavior, as well as the events that occur immediately following the behavior. If the classroom is observed over a period of time, it may be found that certain directions or events always lead to the undesired behavior on the part of the students.

It's important to know the consequence of that behavior. What did you as the teacher do? The response of others to the behavior may be the reason the behavior is repeated over and over. In some way the reaction of others in the room, whether students, teachers, or both, reinforces the student with the undesired behavior enough so that the behavior will be repeated if the opportunity arises again. Thus, the effect on the child or the others' responses is critical in determining whether the behaviors will occur again. If change is to occur, it will be important to change the events occurring just prior to the behaviors so that the behavior will not be elicited, to change both yours and the students' responses to the behaviors if they do occur, and to look at how the responses of others affect the child's particular need for reinforcement.

Sometimes undesired behavior results because the children are unaware of what is expected. All of us need to have limits set, and we are only comfortable when we know what these limits are. When we took our current positions, we wanted to know if there were a dress code for teachers, what time we had to report to work, the length of our teaching day, our responsibilities in the classroom and within the school, and when and how we would receive our paychecks. We wanted to know what was expected, but the fact that we wanted to know when payday was showed our need for reinforcement. Without that reinforcement, how long would our teaching continue?

If we, who have had many different types of experiences, need the limits and structure of our jobs explained and set for us, think of how much greater is the need of inexperienced young students. We can help them in this need by explaining our classroom and school climate and to put these rules in positive rather than negative terms. Thus, "we walk" is much more positive than "we don't run," "stash your trash" more positive than "we don't litter." A general explanation of expected behavior can do much to set the general tone of the classroom and school. In this day of vandalism and destruction, one school has a lobby filled with antiques and halls lined with expensive artwork placed at eye level for the young students. There has been no vandalism; the behavior expected toward these objects has been fully explained and the students have been very willing to provide such behavior. The objects are there for their enjoyment, and they are extremely protective that they not be taken away. Expectations can do much to aid in developing appropriate behaviors.

Some children have a great need for having limitations set for them. This need extends even to the necessity for a definite schedule of activities for them to follow. They are unable to structure their own environment and must rely on others to structure it for them. By following the structure of others, it is hoped that they will learn to structure for themselves.

SEATING

Seating within the classroom can affect the behavior that is seen within the class. When handicapped children are involved, it is particularly important to see that the children are seated in the spot most favorable to them. To seat children on crutches across the room from the entrance so that they must walk through and around the desks will add several minutes to their movements whenever there is a need to move. Children who have mobility problems should be seated near the entrance of the room, as well as near the group setting to which they may need to move within the room. A place needs to be provided for crutches, walkers, and wheelchairs. If that place is within the reach of the children, they will be able to function independently, a goal for all handicapped students. If the children are using crutches, there needs to be a means worked out for carrying books. If the children have excellent balance and movement, a backpack or book bag can be used. If the children are unsure or unstable on crutches, other children can be asked to carry the books to the desired locations. All children should be urged to become as independent as possible, and perhaps you, the children, and the itinerant or resource teacher can come up with ideas to aid their independence.

The blind or partially seeing children who use braille writers or low-vision aids should be seated so that it is easy for them to find their seats. It also should be easy for them to locate their own equipment. They are not encouraged to become independent if they sit down and you bring them their materials. They should learn the location of the materials, how to reach them, to take them back to their seats, and to return them to their proper place before they leave the room. It may mean that you will have to reorganize your classroom after you have had it a particular way for years, but it is important that the children be able to function independently both in and out of the classroom.

Distractible children should receive particularly careful attention when you consider where to seat them. If you put two such children near each other, you can be assured of chaos. One child will stimulate the other, and just when it seems that one child is settling down, the other will do something. A constant problem will result. It is much more practical to plan beforehand to prevent this type of behavior from occurring. Children who are apt to be over-stimulated by others should be placed beside children who are not apt to draw attention to what they are doing. Self-directed, quiet students are much better neighbors, for their activities are less likely to be distracting, and they provide a very good model for restless children.

We have already mentioned that hard of hearing children should be placed near where you will be standing when you give directions, that the light should fall on your face, and that the students should not have to face into the light to try to read your lips. Children with visual and/or auditory problems should be placed so that they are able to read the material that is written on the board. They should also be positioned so that they can unobtrusively get out of their seats and approach the board if they are unable to see what you have written there.

It is also important to structure the classroom so that all of the children in the classroom will create the smallest disturbance possible when they get up to move into small groups, walk to the storage cupboard for supplies, or travel to their lockers to get their coats or lunches. Natural light from the windows, as well as the placement of the blackboards, bulletin boards, and sink, will make a difference in the way in which you arrange your classroom. Before you spend a lot of time and energy rearranging your furniture, you might put the new arrangement on paper and then mark the pathways that each of the students would have to follow to get to the various places in the room. Planning on paper will also help you to separate the children that seem to stimulate each other into behavior that you wish to extinguish. Regrouping for your smaller groups can also be a means of keeping these students apart. Writing things out on paper will help you see possible combinations that may be as explosive as the original situation you are trying to arrest.

SCANNING THE ROOM

Probably the single most effective technique for behavior control is frequent visual scanning of the room. To be a really effective teacher, you must be aware of everything that goes on within the confines of your room at all times. Even though you may have your back turned when you are writing on the blackboard, your ears should be aiding you in determining what is happening.

Scanning the room takes practice, but it can be learned in a short time and is extremely effective in controlling the behavior of the children. It involves visually scanning the room every couple of minutes, no matter what the activity in which you are engaged. If sitting at the front of the room with a small group, your chair should be placed so that you can pay attention to the group you are working with, but you can also visually scan the room to see what the other children are doing. Often children who are just conceiving an idea for some type of deviltry get back to work when they are aware that the teacher is keeping tabs on their behavior. Scanning allows the teacher to intervene before children carry out their behaviors. If such children get out of their seats, the teacher can remind them to get back in before they get into difficulty.

Eye contact is an important action to use during the scanning procedure. As the children begin to look around, an antecedent for most children who get themselves into trouble in the classroom, those children will encounter your eyes as part of their search. This contact is usually enough to get them back to the task they are supposed to be doing. Most of the time, that will be all that is needed. No words need to be spoken. The children see that you are observing and get back to the task at hand.

By scanning the room you will also be able to interfere in children's intentions of doing something that is not allowed. If children get up from their desks to go over to the library bookcase, you can remind them that now is not the time that they are allowed to do that activity unless their work is finished. Such interference works well with the type of children who need particular control, if given when they get the "look" or begin the antecedent behavior that in the past has always led to trouble. By getting to the children and breaking into their usual chain of behavior, you can often prevent the consequences of that behavior. As the children are able to gain more and more control over their own behavior, the interference will become less and less needed, and you will be able to fade such help.

If you are not engaged in a group session or working individually with another student, it is a good idea to walk about the classroom. In your scanning, you may observe children who show behavior that eye contact alone cannot control. Children who are engaged in a subject that is difficult will often start to fidget, look about the room, lean over to whisper to a neighbor, and so on, and it is at this time that walking about the room can allow you to move close to those who are demonstrating this type of behavior. Your moving close to them may be all that is needed to control their behavior and allow them to keep on task. Merely being close will give such children enough direction and control that the task can be completed.

Sometimes even your presence near the children will not be enough to control their behavior. Touching them may be needed. A pat on the back, while telling them that they are doing a good job, to keep going, that they're almost finished, and so forth, will be necessary to get them back or to keep them on the task at hand. This technique also works on the playground when there are two children who are just about to lose control of themselves and enter into a fist fight. By stepping between the children and placing your arms around each of their shoulders and talking quietly to them, you give the control that they are lacking and allow their tempers to cool down until they can provide their own control.

By moving around the room you will also be able to spot those who are having particular problems with their work. Walking up to them and pausing to look at their work and, gaining eye contact, nodding and showing them that they are doing a good job will often be all that is needed for them to go on with their work. Touching the children by patting them on their backs also aids them at the point when they are having trouble. Speaking to them may also help them hurdle the problem they are having. Praise for completing as much as has been done also works. Words of encouragement which show that you care can do much. "You've done such a good job so far with your problems. Let's see if you can finish them," can be much more effective than, "You haven't finished your work." Standing next to the children who look as if they are having difficulty long enough to spot that difficulty may also be helpful. Recognizing the fact that the children have forgotten to borrow when subtracting can aid you in directing them through the correct steps, giving them any information that was forgotten or not learned.

By helping the children in these ways, the outbursts that come from sheer frustration can be prevented. The actions of children who crumple their papers into balls and throw them into the basket because of frustration in not being able to complete the last problem can be eliminated. The children who have such an outburst often cannot be talked into doing all of the problems again and will take a low mark for a missing paper rather than do all the work over. Helping such children at the time they need it can prevent such outbursts and can often raise their grades because they are able to turn in completed papers.

Sometimes scanning the room or establishing eye contact with the children who are about to get themselves into difficulty may not be effective. For these children, directly confronting them with what they are about to do and how it will lead them into trouble may work. Children who lack a great deal of control and who are unable to see the consequences of their behavior in terms of the long range may be helped by carefully discussing the possible end effect with them. A carefully planned program for helping such children increase their ability to see such consequences can be implemented over time and can be as successful as planning a long-term arithmetic program can be effective in that subject.

Scanning the room can also help in spotting the children who are preoccupied with the teaching materials or other objects that have been assigned or that they have taken out of their pockets or desks. If eye contact or walking over to them has not resulted in the behavior you desire, it may be necessary to remove the objects from them. If this is necessary, you will need to have some type of rules in your classroom for objects that are removed from the children. Rubber bands and marbles are different than brass knuckles and switch blades, and you need to have thought out beforehand what rules you will have for both types of materials.

PLANNED IGNORING

When we ask for help regarding students who are extremely disruptive with their behavior, we often get the advice to "ignore it." Ignoring behavior needs to be carefully planned, however, or it can result in reinforcing a child's behavior instead of extinguishing it. Let us look for a minute at the principles of reinforcement. Most of us, when we begin to teach an activity, use a one-to-one reinforcement schedule. The children respond correctly and we reward in some manner. The children respond again and we reward again. This is the weakest reinforcement there is, for the children learn that when they do something, they are rewarded each time they do it. Therefore, we have to try to get the children on some other type of reinforcement schedule. If not, they will try something once and if not rewarded, will perhaps try again. If not rewarded the second time, however, they will often stop trying. How many of us will put money into a Coke machine after not getting a coke the first or second time?

If we reward the second time the children perform an activity, the children soon learn that they must do something two times before receiving a reward. After a while we switch to three performances before rewarding and eventually to an intermittent reinforcement schedule in which we want the children to continue on for quite awhile, knowing that sooner or later the reinforcement will come. Most of us will not continue indefinitely, however. If we happened to not get our monetary reinforcement as teachers, how long would we continue teaching? If that reinforcement comes at the end of each week, we would probably not continue teaching as long as those whose reinforcements come twice a month or those who get paid once a month.

Schedules of reinforcement must also be considered when we decide to ignore behavior. If children are doing something to get attention and we decide to ignore them, we must think through the complete consequences of that ignoring. Let's say that we have decided to ignore a male student who often gets out of his seat and wanders about the classroom, getting into trouble. We see the child get up, and we decide to ignore him. Through our scanning of the room we know that he is walking around the classroom, and we again decide to ignore him. We see him go up to another child and brush against that child, but we continue to ignore him. We watch as he goes up to another child and gives that child a slight push; we grit our teeth as we tell ourselves that we *will* ignore him. He then goes to another child and pushes hard enough to knock that child to the floor. It is at this point that we finally decide we cannot ignore behavior that might harm others, and we yell at the child to get back in his seat. At this point we are reinforcing the child on an intermittent reinforcement schedule. The child finally got the attention that he wanted and has now been reinforced so that next time he will continue his nonconforming behavior for an even longer period of time. Thus, we have not ignored him, but have made his behavior even stronger over the long run.

Because of this type of reinforcement, we must consider the total long-term consequences of ignoring behavior and decide if we can ignore such behavior. One study was done with mothers and their exceptional children, and it was found that the mothers who ignored the demands of their children had children who were more whining and demanding than those mothers who outright told their children that they would not help them. Ignoring behavior, then, must be used with discretion. Cognizance of the long-range effects should make all of us use it infrequently but well.

REMOVAL FROM THE GROUP

Removal from the group is another technique that can backfire on a teacher who uses it without thinking through all of its ramifications. Sending children into the hall can result in greater reinforcement than keeping those children in the room. Children who are in a busy hallway get to see everything that is going on. Teachers and students may come up to them and ask why they are there. The principal may do the same. Think of all the attention those children are getting!

A much more effective removal is to a location where there is no reinforcement. Children can be turned from the group and allowed to have no interaction with the group. Removal to another part of the room can also be effective *if* there is nothing around to reward the children for being sent there. Sometimes the reactions of the other children can be rewarding to the children who are removed. Comments on the playground regarding the behavior may be all that is needed to keep the children repeating the activity that caused the removal. Judicious use of removal becomes extremely important to a teacher desiring a well-run classroom.

PHYSICAL RESTRAINT

Physical restraint should be the least used management device. It is used only for those children who completely break down and need some kind of restraint to keep them from hurting themselves or others. Children who go into temper tantrums and hit their heads against the wall or floor until they bleed may be the type who need it.

Physical restraint is used because the children are not able to control their own behavior. If you use physical restraint, be careful in how you restrain the children. Folding your arms around theirs and keeping your arms away from their mouths can do much to prevent bites to you and to themselves. Holding them slightly to one side of you so that they cannot kick you protects you from those who are completely out of control. Holding the children to the side also aids you in control if you can use one arm across them to control both of their arms. That will leave you one arm free to aid in other ways.

On-the-floor restraint is also possible. Straddling the children will allow you to use your total body for restraint. Children who are larger than you can effectively be restrained in this manner. You should never hold children in anger. If you are angry, your body will communicate this to the children. Restraint is not for angry people, it is to help the children when they lose self-control. Talking quietly to the children while restraining them will also help them to understand that you are trying to help rather than punish. When you are holding them tightly, you can feel the tenseness flow from their bodies and can usually tell when it is safe to release them. If letting up slightly on your hold brings increased resistance from them, it may be necessary to increase your hold again, talking calmly to let them know that you are in control and that they can depend on you for this. Most classroom teachers will never have to hold a child in restraint in the course of their complete teaching careers. However, it is nice to know the techniques so that if the rare occasion arises, you will know what to do.

CHAPTER 15
CLASSROOM AIDES

Keeping an eye on a large group of children while still making sure that they are learning while you are doing it is a difficult task. Adding children who have special problems to that group makes it even more difficult. However, there are many techniques that can be used to help in this task. We have discussed many of them. The use of other people can also aid you in this endeavor.

Parents should never be overlooked as extra hands when working with children. We as teachers often think of asking parents to help us when we make school trips but don't think of them for day-to-day assistance. Some parents, if contacted, are more than willing to come to school at specific times to aid us in a particular task. Children who are mainstreamed will often have parents who are very grateful and will be more than willing to assist us. However, you will find that some parents are really not very good in the classroom and some children will react negatively to their parents being in school. Those same parents may be able to grade papers, make materials, and create bulletin boards so that your time will be freed for other activities, however.

Volunteers are also a great deal of help. Both parents and volunteers will have to be trained, but many will stay with you for years, and the time you spend can be very worthwhile. A notice in the community paper, the school newsletter, or church bulletin are all means to let the public know that you are in need of help for your classroom. Volunteers can often be used for the maintenance and transfer stages of learning an activity. Some volunteers will be extremely creative and will have excellent ideas for activities for these stages.

Classroom teaching aides that are paid for by the school board are another source of help, if the teaching task begins to become too much. Some schools hire aides for such items as collecting lunch and milk money, taking attendance, monitoring the halls and bathrooms, and so forth. In these days of economic crunch, it is best not to plan on such help, however. If we have them, fine. If not, the use of parents and volunteers will have to suffice. The efficient use of any classroom aide can do much to give additional teaching time.

No matter whether your classroom aide is a parent, a paid aide, a volunteer, or students from upper grades, he or she needs some type of orientation to your class. Any type of aide can commit havoc within your room by permitting behavior that is not allowed, by encouraging the children to finish their work one way when you have carefully built up another way of doing it, and by reacting as a poor model to your handicapped children. To make good use of aides, then, it is important that some means be found for you to share specific information about your classroom. You might ask them to observe you and your children for a day to see if they are truly interested in acting as an aide. This period of observation is important, for it means that time will not be spent in training if the potential person has a personality conflict with you or if some of the children or behaviors in the classroom are such that the person would not be able to work with them throughout the day.

If the initial visit has worked out well and the person is still interested, it will be necessary for you to set aside specific time for training and orientation to the room and children. This training and orientation might take place before or after school, during conversation over lunch, or as part of your planning periods. During the orientation, there are many things that need to be covered about the school in general. For example, the general philosophy of the school administrator and the administrative structure within the school should be discussed so that people and their responsibilities within the school are noted. Thus, during any absence that you might have in the future, the aide can inform the substitute teacher who might appear on the scene and need some type of help in this area. The physical plant information should also be covered. The location of the lunchroom, playground, office, teacher's lounge, and so forth, will be important to all aides in the classroom if they will be there throughout the day and take an active part in your scheduling. Of particular importance are the locations of the resource, speech, occupational and physical therapy rooms if the handicapped children in your room attend one of those, and the aide is responsible for taking the children there.

Rules that must be adhered to should also be pointed out, so that your aide is aware of those that are part of the total school environment. Such things might include any particular rules relating to the administration of the building: fire drills and where the children are to go when in the various places they might be found throughout the day; procedures that must be followed in the event the aide is absent as well as the aide's responsibility if you should happen to be ill; procedures for parking on and off the grounds; phone calls; playground responsibilities; procedures for leaving class; use of various pieces of equipment, the storage, permission, operation, and the process to use if there is some type of replacement necessary; and payday, if appropriate.

You will also need to cover your own classroom in great detail, going into your own personal philosophy; the administrative structure that you use within the class; the physical set-up that you use and why it is necessary, particularly for the handicapped children within your class; any special classes or activities that the children in the room attend and their locations; the rules and duties for the children as well as for the aides; emergency and safety procedures; treatment of visitors; and procedures to follow in the event of illness during the day by children, teacher, or the aide. Lunch procedures are important. Who stays with the children during lunch? Do you have a separate time for lunch or do you eat with the children? Will the aide be responsible for any of the lunchroom activities? When will the aide eat, and where? The length of a day is vital information and the hours that you expect the aide in the classroom should be communicated. Responsibilities of the aide and the manner in which you want them carried out are important pieces of information. A discussion of the type of climate you try to create within the classroom; the types of rewards you use and the frequency you use them; and the types of discipline that you expect the aide to use as well as the procedures to follow if that discipline is not maintained will prevent inconsistencies.

You also want to inform the aide of the location of supplies within the classroom and the means to obtain other supplies if there are none in the room; also the location of the children's lavatories, the nurses' station, playground equipment, and first aid materials. You also want to inform the aide of times during the day when you will be away from the classroom as well as the time that will be set aside for breaks for the aide. Playground responsibilities should be reviewed.

You will also want your aide to know the general background of the children within your class, their general SES, length of time within the program if there are any children who are new to your room and might not be familiar with all of your rules and procedures, whether the children are bussed or walk from the neighborhood, your attitudes towards them, and your expectations regarding their behavior. Any medical problems should be pointed out as well as the classroom procedures to be followed if any of the children exhibit symptoms during class, and any positioning, toileting procedures, and programs and methods should be discussed. A general introduction to terms that are used in the classroom; confidentiality of information about the children in the room; special equipment, materials, supplies, their locations, and the ways that they are to be used; the curriculum and the programs for each of the children and the methods that you use to teach them; specific classroom procedures such as your method for charting the behaviors of the children; your behavior management system; the means of communication that must be used with the children; and what the aide is to do if a parent walks into class should all be addressed. You may want to put some of the general information into a typed paper so that the information can be reviewed periodically with the aide. Such information is also invaluable to a substitute when one is necessary.

No matter what type of aide you have in your class, it is important that you keep open the lines of communication between you. If the aide exhibits behavior that you think inappropriate, immediately inform him or her. Do not do it in such a way that the aide is embarrassed or so the children interpret your actions to mean they do not have to respond. Support your aide in interaction with the children, and let the children know they must carry out the aide's instructions. Any differences of opinion can be aired when the children are not present. Otherwise, the children will soon attempt to pit the aide against you. The more thoroughly informed the aides are about what you want to occur in the classroom, the more they can act in concert with you for the good of the children.

Even though there may be no parents, volunteers, or aides to help you in the classroom, there is an excellent source of frequently untapped help—the children in the classroom. Peer help has been mentioned before, and it is an excellent means of giving additional aid to the children who need it. Peers can often help others in the initial acquisition stages of learning if they themselves are in the maintenance or generalization stages. Even the child who has very slowly learned a task can gain much from helping a child who is even more slow. Many teachers have decided on their career goals after they were chosen to help others with their learning tasks.

Sometimes the use of other children can aid in the teacher-child interaction. Some children may not yet be ready for the type of interaction desired. Children who are ready can be used. Johnny may be extremely sensitive about his problems with arithmetic. He is aware that the teacher knows he doesn't know, but he wants to protect himself from the teacher knowing the extent of his ignorance. Thus, the teacher, who may or may not be cognizant of his shortcomings, becomes unapproachable. A peer or cross-age tutor is much less threatening to the child, and Johnny will be much more likely to be open to assistance from this source. This is true of children from first grade through graduate school. Although they may not be steeped in pedagogy, peer or cross-age tutors can often explain things more clearly than the teacher. They can communicate the process in their own terminology. Sometimes peer tutors will relate how they themselves have thought things through to make sense of them, thus communicating to the children a particular means to process the material.

We have earlier discussed how some children benefit from working through a problem aloud. By listening we can determine the process they are using to arrive at the answers. This process works particularly well for arithmetic problems, for when the children verbalize what they are doing at each step, we can pinpoint the exact place where they are having difficulty. Because we, as teachers, may not have the time to hear each of our children verbalize the steps they are taking, assigning a peer for this purpose can be equally effective. Having an area of the room arranged so that the children can work side by side will isolate them somewhat from the other children so that they will be less distracting. Again, the peer who is being used for such tutoring should be in the maintenance or generalization stages of learning acquisition for greatest effectiveness.

We have just reviewed the means by which a carefully structured classroom setting can aid us in our educational endeavors. We have looked at the children and the problems they bring to us because of their handicapping conditions, the means by which we might plan and implement the tasks that we need to teach them, and how the setting can be planned to effect learning positively.

These were the means originally discussed as enabling us to work effectively with children with special needs who have been mainstreamed into our classroom. However, there will be questions that will arise when examining the children, the task, or the setting for which we'd like additional information. Part V offers various resources available to those who educate exceptional children.

PART 5
RESOURCES FOR THE CLASSROOM TEACHER

When we begin a new adventure, we like to be assured that there is some safety factor involved that will get us out of any trouble that we may encounter. Teachers who are mainstreaming their first exceptional learner feel the same way. "I'll try. But you'll have to help me if I need it," is a common expression heard when the subject of taking on such a responsibility is discussed. There are support systems available to the classroom teacher, and we should be aware of all of them. P.L. 94–142 contains several such supports, and we need to know what they are and how to use them effectively.

CHAPTER 16
SPECIAL EDUCATION
SUPPORT SERVICES

A look at the children's folders can help you determine the support systems that have been decided upon for particular children. If the i.e.p. states that the children are to have certain types of additional help during the school year, you should be aware of them. Obtaining that particular help should not be your responsibility, although it may be your charge to see that the children are reminded to go somewhere else in the building for some type of education or therapy.

As part of your school's P.L. 94–142 plan, there should be some type of monitoring mechanism to see that the services stipulated in the i.e.p.'s are being provided. If they are not, you should contact the special education personnel assigned to your children and the responsible administrative individuals who have been made accountable for this. This is part of your role as an advocate for the children. As their teacher, you also want them to make as much progress as they can. Services specified in the i.e.p. are to be provided because they were felt vital to the handicapped children's level of functioning. Therefore, the children should be receiving them.

The program in special education within your system should also have a ready support system for regular teachers who have mainstreamed children in their classroom even part of the day. Some schools have resource rooms where there is a teacher of exceptional children available throughout the day. Children can be sent to these rooms for tutoring, testing, crisis care, and so on. You need to become familiar with this teacher and the role that has been determined for that teacher within the confines of your school. Resource rooms are usually used for short, specified periods for intensive academic remediation and/or control of problem behaviors.

Resource rooms can be staffed by various types of support personnel. It is important that you learn the background of the person staffing yours so that you will know the type of support that you can expect from that person.

The person in charge of the resource room might be an elementary or secondary teacher who has exhibited excellent teaching skills and has been rewarded by being placed in a room where those skills can be used by other teachers. Skilled in handling problems in teaching children, these teachers may be very good in providing information about teaching tasks and managing children in various types of settings. They may know very little about special education, however, and it will be necessary for you to seek out other help if the information you want is in the area of some problem the child has as a result of a handicapping condition.

Or, the resource room teacher may be a person that was teaching a self-contained class prior to the implementation of P.L. 94–142. If that is the case, the teacher will probably have a great deal of information about one specific type of handicapping condition, or perhaps two if she or he has been teaching for some period of time. If lacking information about the type of handicap one of your children is exhibiting, the teacher should be able to obtain the information you seek, either by having a familiarity with the literature and personnel or knowing the resources for obtaining such information.

The resource teacher may also have been prepared in a generic special education preparation program. These programs, now in vogue, have resulted because the labels of handicapping conditions often have made little difference in the means by which the children are taught. Although the handicapping conditions may vary, the teaching procedures may be the same. A person trained in this manner should be aware of the various implications of specific types of handicapping conditions and will be more likely to be of immediate help if you need specific information regarding a particular handicapping condition.

Some schools do not have resource room teachers but will have itinerant teachers who will visit your building on a regular schedule. You need to become knowledgeable about that schedule and how to get in touch with the teacher so that you can ask for materials, advice, or assistance between visits as well as during scheduled visits.

It is important that the two of you find time in your busy schedules to communicate about the children. When the teacher sets up the original schedules for seeing them, allowing time to discuss matters should be considered. Your prep times, lunch time, recess, seatwork time, and so on should be given to the itinerant teacher to note so that you will not have to listen with one ear to that teacher while your reading group waits for you to finish.

Time for communication between you and the special education personnel is just as important as time between that teacher and your children. If you are aware of what is being taught in the children's resource room or itinerant periods, you will be more able to extend those activities or practices into the classroom for proficiency and generalization. Talking with the special education teacher while you are on hall duty, during recess, or while your children are gone for other classes is a better time than while they are all in the room. If you feel children really miss too much when they leave your room for their special education services, you should communicate that fact. Sometimes it is possible for the special education teachers to work with them during times when they are normally in "down time," that is, waiting for their busses or cabs. The tight schedules of itinerant personnel may mean that you will never have time to see them while they are in the building. A sharing of schedules will allow you to find mutual times when phone conversations can be held.

For some types of information or some needs of the children, it may be possible for the consultant or itinerant to use the time normally used in seeing the children on a one-to-one basis in the regular classroom. Time spent in the classroom showing you how to incorporate speech activities into your routine, how to respond to a child who has very little intelligible speech, or how to position a severely handicapped child can all be used to great advantage. You can then continue these activities on the days when the child is not being seen by the specialist. You might ask the special teachers that your children have to provide you with such services.

The role of consulting teacher has received increased emphasis since the implementation of P.L. 94-142. This teacher is to work primarily with classroom teachers rather than doing direct work with children. Because this teacher devotes all of the day to individual teachers, helping them with problems of mainstreaming specific children within a building, you can usually schedule meetings on a regular basis. Such a teacher's responsibilities also include consultation on a crisis basis, even if that time is not regularly scheduled.

Children may also be assigned to your class from a self-contained special education setting. Such children usually are in the initial stages of mainstreaming. As the year progresses, the amount of time in the regular class usually increases. The children's special education teachers will be the source of support for those specific children. Specific times for communication with these teachers can be arranged during your initial contacts with them.

During your conversations with the special education personnel you should feel free to discuss any and all concerns that you have regarding your children. Some teachers will have had considerable experience and will be full of assistance. Others won't be quite as helpful. Some will be teachers of special education classes whose children are currently all mainstreamed and who have been assigned to resource, itinerant, or consultant positions. Others have been trained specifically for their present tasks. Regardless of their backgrounds, it is important that you grow together in the ability to mainstream children successfully. Open communication will aid in this task.

When looking for support services for advice, don't overlook other personnel within your own building. Principals, counselors, and fellow teachers may be able to make suggestions based upon their prior experiences. Even the librarian can be of help in suggesting references for you or bibliotherapy for the children. What has worked for different people in the past may be very appropriate for your current students. The old W-W principle comes into play here. The source of help or the type of activity suggested is not important. It's W-W, whatever works.

CHAPTER 17
PARENTAL INVOLVEMENT

Parents are one of the most frequently overlooked resources that teachers can use. They can also be the most helpful. Actually knowing how to approach parents can be a difficult matter. Even minor encounters may be awkward, for most of us have had very little training in working with parents, and we are most hesitant in approaching them. Even those of us who have children may be extremely hesitant in dealing with other parents. The presence of the unknown in what particular parents may contribute or not contribute presents a problem to us.

Most of us look forward to sessions with parents who have proven particularly helpful to us in the past. A session with such parents can be truly stimulating, for they become true members of the team and we feel that part of our job becomes easier, knowing that the parents are assuming part of the responsibility for their own children. We then know that there is some type of carry-over between the home and the school, and that success will be more assured with such cooperation.

Not all parents are capable of helping in the same manner that we would like them to help. Some have had very unpleasant school experiences and hate to be called to school for any reason because it brings back so many unpleasant memories. Others feel that the teacher and school system in general have something against their particular children and that meetings will result in unpleasantness no matter what the outcome. Others have only been called to school when something unpleasant has happened, and so they associate a conference with hearing more unpleasant details regarding their children. Other parents demand more services than the school is capable of providing. They want their children to be provided with a maximum of every service available, even though such service may not be indicated.

Some parents are so uninformed about their own children that they may be of little help in setting goals for them. Others are so limited themselves that they can be of little help in advancing their children. Yet we must work with all of them particularly when we sit down to plan their children's i.e.p.'s. We may receive a great deal of help from some and very little from others. All must be involved, however.

Most of us feel very comfortable dealing with middle-class parents who have had backgrounds similar to ours. Many of the parents who have a college background seem particularly easy to talk to because they understand our vocabularies and know the long-term value of a good education. Most of them will be very aware of the need to complete as much education as possible and to have the children reach their highest level of attainment.

Some of these parents, however, may have a lot of emotional problems in dealing with their children's exceptionality. A father who has worked his way through college and medical school may be determined that his child will have it much easier when that child goes through medical school. The father plans carefully for the financial security of his children to ensure a higher education and then finds that the child he had designated to be a medical partner is in fact retarded. A great deal of sympathy and empathy need to be given to such parents when the child is discussed. Facts must be kept as facts, however, and emotions should not get in the way of presenting pertinent facts to the parents and in developing good, relevant programs. That is not to say that there is no kindness shown to the parents. Kindness should be an integral part of dealing with all the parents of all the children.

Teachers usually find it much more easy to deal with people from a very open social network within our society. Such an open network promotes the referral of children to resources within the community to pinpoint the problems they are having and for locating remedial personnel for dealing with them. Let's take, for example, two mothers who come to you for conferences in dealing with the problems their sons are having in the school setting. When the first mother, a member of a very open network, appears for a conference, you tell her that you are very concerned about her son's progress, that his work has steadily decreased in amount and accuracy. You wonder if there is something you should know about the child to aid in understanding his problems. The mother breaks down and proceeds to tell you that her husband has become an alcoholic and that this fact is disrupting the whole family. The husband comes home drunk every night and then proceeds to fight with his wife. The noise keeps the children awake and frightens them. They have become not only terrified of their father in his drunken state, but are also full of fear for their own futures, their safety, and the safety of their mother.

After hearing this story you gently inquire whether the mother has sought help for her plight and whether the husband has considered AA. The mother reports that she has been too ashamed to seek help and that her husband has refused all thoughts of AA, refusing to admit that he has a problem. Before your conference is over, however, you have talked the mother into attending the meetings for spouses of alcoholics, into sending her teenagers to a meeting specifically for them, and to referring her son to the school social worker for help in dealing with his problems. You both end the meeting feeling very good. Your knowledge of resources has aided the mother in helping to find help for her problems, and the mother's open reception to accepting services within the community has aided her in getting needed help.

The second mother is a different matter, however. She is a member of a closed social network and is not receptive to seeking help from outside sources. Although many members of closed networks have at some time sought help from such sources, these experiences have invariably resulted in failure because we who are members of an open social network fail to understand and meet the needs of those members of the closed network with whom we've dealt.

The teacher mentions to the second mother that her son is experiencing a great deal of difficulty in his schoolwork. The mother says that she , too, has noticed this and that every time her son has brought home a paper with a poor grade on it, she has given him a beating, but these beatings just haven't done any good. You, horrified that the grades that you have given to the boy have resulted in his being beaten, try another approach. You suggest that there may be something troubling the boy and that by getting to the source of the problem, the boy's performance may improve. The mother at this point confides that her husband has become an alcoholic and that he comes home each night and beats her. She adds that the children get little sleep because the fights last most of the night and the noise keeps them awake.

At this point you ask the mother whether or not her husband has thought of joining AA. She responds that he refuses to admit that he has a problem. The mother relates that she has tried to take care of the problem by locating all of the hiding places where her husband keeps his bottles. She tells of finding each one and how over a period of time she has poured out the contents of each bottle. This act has only infuriated her husband, and he has beaten her even more. He also has continued to bring home other bottles and the overall effect of her actions on his drinking has been nil. The mother then states in a very resigned manner that she has given up on her husband as well as on her son. She has tried her best, but this has done no good and so she feels that the problems are something that she has to learn to live with.

The fatalistic attitude bothers you. You, as an open network person, do not understand this, and you continue to make suggestions to the mother based upon your open network knowledge of resources. The mother refuses to accept the suggestions, and you close the conference with a great feeling of frustration. You relate to the principal that the mother was uncooperative and not interested in the problems her son presented.

In truth, the mother is very interested in her son's problems and would very much like a solution to them, as well as to her own. However, the solutions that have been offered have been those acceptable to members of an open network. She is not such a person and has long ago learned to distrust such persons and agencies. She, as a member of a closed network, has learned that only those within that network can be trusted. If you had realized this, your recommendations could have been much more relevant to her needs.

Closed network persons have learned which persons within their own closed network that they can trust. There is usually someone within that network who is very intelligent and has a great amount of common sense. Although this individual is usually not well educated (education usually changes one from a closed network person to an open network person), the individual usually is able to offer suggestions for dealing with the problems. Such a person may be a grandmother who has learned much from a very hard life and is able to help others profit from her experiences, an aunt who is an "aunt" to everyone regardless of kinship, or it may be the wise woman on the block who helps whomever comes to her with problems. Perhaps this is the type of person who can help the mother you are working with to deal with her problems. Sometimes members of a closed network bring such highly regarded people with them when they have their school conferences. That person may later be able to help the mother with her problems because of the information gained during the conference. Thus it is important to remember that we all are not similarly impressed with what resources in the community can do to aid us.

It is also important to remember that there are some resources within the area that cater to members of a closed network. People within that network have educated themselves to be of aid and have established resources run by members of the closed network and designed to help others of that network. By becoming aware of those resources, you can aid the parents who are in need of services by making them aware of resources that they can accept according to their own backgrounds.

Parents can do much to aid us in developing a good program for the children we teach. We work with the children for several hours each day and see them in a very structured setting. We often have no idea of the behavior of the children in other settings. Only by communicating with parents can we learn how much what we are teaching is transferred into their everyday lives. Only by cooperating and communicating with the parents can we set up a 24-hour day program so that our handicapped children will learn to function to the best of their ability in their total life settings.

It may mean that we have to change the vocabulary that we use to get our points across to the parents. It may mean taking great efforts to establish a trusting relationship with people who have very little education but are much more effective with their own children than we as teachers will ever be. It will mean continuing to grow in our relationships with others.

Sometimes little things turn parents off. A tone of voice that appears too authoritarian. Talking down to the parents in our efforts to communicate with them. One parent put it very well as she discussed her new social worker with the teacher who came to tutor her exceptional child. "She drives a car like yours, but she's not like you." When asked how the teacher and social worker differed, the mother remarked with sarcasm in her voice, "*She* locks her car before coming into the house." How often we must unconsciously relay information that can be misinterpreted by others. Only by establishing an open relationship with our parents can we learn the things that lead to misunderstandings. Only through sincere efforts to work with parents can a relationship be built on trust and mutual admiration.

There are other factors to consider while working with the parents of the children in your room. Every parent comes to you with strengths and weaknesses that are a part of being human. Some parents will be easy to work with, while others will be very difficult. When teaching, we do not "give up" on the difficult children, and so we should not give up on the difficult parents. Sometimes their difficulties are the result of a lack of understanding or of previous unpleasant experiences with teachers. Some may be a result of the parent's own frustrations with education. Whatever the reason, and we may never learn what it is, we need to approach each parent with the same sense of dedication that we use with that parent's child.

All parents come with different backgrounds, experiences, and expectations for their children. It is important to know as much as possible regarding these things so that we can put the information we wish to give to them in terms that they can understand. We have learned our "educationalese" through prolonged formal and informal exposure to it. If you have forgotten how much this educationalese has become a part of you, go back through the notes that were taken in some of your courses. Since we normally do not write down the information that is already known to us, we are quite often surprised at the number of notes taken and at our current familiarity with information that was unknown to us not too long ago.

Some parents will come to us with the same type of background that we have, and professional terms may be used during discussions with those parents. Others parents will be interested enough to seek out information regarding their children and will be as familiar as we regarding educational terms. Some parents may be even more informed than we about the nature of their children's handicapping condition, the prognoses, and the ways in which they should be handled in the classroom. These parents can do much to educate us, and it is vital that we listen and learn from such well-educated sources.

Not all parents will come to us with this type of background, however. In fact, that type of parent will be in the minority, and the rest will need much more help from us. It is important that we have some idea of where to place our vocabulary level when talking to a parent. A few comments or questions that elicit conversation from the parent will sometimes help to determine the level of vocabulary and approximate background. By gearing our conversation to the same level, we should be able to communicate the information that we wish. The parent who lacks the type of background we have may be more difficult to communicate with if we fail to remember that everything we say to that parent should be put at a level that can be understood by someone having no experience in the area.

One example brings to mind the misconcepts that can arise because of a lack of communication between parent and teacher. A teacher who was just beginning work with a young child called to report to the director that the mother seemed extremely passive and disinterested in what was being planned for her child. The grandmother, who made her home with them, also seemed to be indifferent to suggestions that were being given. An interview was set up with the director of the program, and information was gathered about the mother and grandmother. During the meeting between the director, mother, and grandmother, the discussion was placed on a rather high level due to the fact that the gathered information reported the mother to be a high school graduate. It was observed that the mother seemed interested but reluctant to answer all questions. At one point it was asked how the child demonstrated the use of imagination. Neither the mother nor the grandmother understood the term and, to their credit, admitted it. This admission brought the conversation to a much more basic use of vocabulary and even then, both admitted that they did not understand several words of the vocabulary used.

Following the interview, the director talked with the teacher involved and suggested to her that she use extremely simple vocabulary with many examples and that she should model any behavior that she wished the parent and grandmother to use with the child. This was done and proved immediately successful. Thus, a mother who was referred to as an "uncooperative" parent became one of the best models in the program. Her child reflected her growing abilities and made significant gains within a very short time. It is important to remember that the parents may be very interested and willing to be cooperative but our inability to communicate with them may prevent them from becoming the type of parents that both we and they would like them to become.

It is also important that we not overload the parents with what we ask them to do. A mother who works all day and has dinner to prepare, children to bathe, clothes to wash and iron, and shopping to do each evening will not approach the request to spend a half hour each day tutoring a child with the same enthusiasm as will the mother who is home all day and looking for something to do with her time. We, as working people, know what it's like to have more work given to us for our evening's activity. Many mothers have more responsibilities and fewer resources than we. We can't blame them if they're unenthusiastic.

It is important to know that not all parents are willing or able to work effectively with their own children. If you have children of your own, ask yourself if you could teach them within your own classroom, if you would be willing to teach them to play the piano, sew a dress or shirt, or carve a bar of soap. Excellent teachers will frequently admit that they are unwilling to teach their own children to drive or to carry out similar activities. This inability should not be seen as a reflection on their parenting ability but accepted as part of individual differences.

Mothers can be used very successfully within the classroom as aides in activities such as tutoring children or overseeing the maintenance and generalization stages of acquisition of specific tasks. It may be possible for mothers who cannot work with their own children to be allowed to work with other children, or to have a mother who is good at tutoring children carry out that activity while another mother who is not good at it becomes involved with other kinds of activities that are just as necessary for successful operation of a classroom. Many are the mothers who have no success in tutoring theirs or other children who are able to answer the office phone, type up messages, or volunteer as escorts during a school trip. All of us come equipped with differing abilities, and they should be expressed, tolerated, and encouraged. It is up to us as teachers to help develop the parents' abilities to become even better parents, not to be seen as criticizing, onmipotent beings.

CHAPTER 18
NATIONAL AND REGIONAL RESOURCES

The U.S. Congress has set up a nationwide support system in the form of regional resource centers that have been established to provide special materials and equipment for exceptional children. The special education teacher serving the children in your room should be able to provide you with the location of the center serving your school and how you can make use of it. Some centers have a central location from which materials can be obtained. Some deliver to your door, some mail materials to you, and some insist that you go to them to pick up what you want. You should find out the types of services provided and become familiar with the materials and equipment that the center has available to you. If you have a very limited materials budget, using those from the center and evaluating their effectiveness can often help you spend your money wisely. How often we have spent a lot of money on a particular material, only to find that it was completely inappropriate to the needs of our children.

Materials that are needed to help exceptional children keep up with their more normal peers should be available for your use. Although you may be able to provide such materials for arithmetic aids as straws, toothpicks, and poker chips, other aids such as demonstration boards and devices; place value materials; colored beads, blocks, rods, discs, number lines, cards and charts; puzzles; and special computational devices such as calculators and other equipment may be available to you for the asking. To be the best teacher for the special children within your room, you should be familiar with the types of material available and make use of them. Speech and language kits, socialization materials, reading series, various types of media packages, instructional sequences in subject areas, and so forth are available through many of the centers. The centers even have kits that you can use for familiarization to handicapping conditions, P.L. 94–142, i.e.p.'s, mainstreaming, and so on. Such kits may be family oriented, peer targeted, or devoted to the handicapped children themselves. Some centers will run computer searches to find the types of appropriate materials for your children. Different kinds of special education reference books are also available.

A visit to some of the centers is like a visit to Santa's workshop at Christmas. The materials are there to make your task of educating exceptional children easier. Borrowing and making use of the materials can aid you with this. Addresses of some of the regional centers follow. Federal support for these centers changes from funding cycle to cycle. To receive information about which centers are operating within your region, you might contact one of the following or your state department of special education.

REGIONAL RESOURCE CENTERS

Northwest Regional Resource Center
Dr. Larry B. Carlson, Acting Director
Clinical Service Building, Third Floor
1590 Willamette Street
University of Oregon
Eugene, Oregon 97401
AC 503-686-5641
      687-6544
FTS   425-6544
Norman Howe, Project Officer

States served:
Alaska, Hawaii,
Samoa, Guam,
Trust Territory
Washington, Idaho,
Oregon, Montana,
Wyoming

California Regional Resource Center
Dr. Judy Grayson, Director
600 South Commonwealth Avenue
Suite 1304
University of Southern California
Los Angeles, California 90005
AC 213-381-5231
FTS 798-4068 or 4069
Norman Howe, Project Officer

States served:
California

Southwest Regional Resource Center
Dr. Wayne Johnson, Director
2363 Foothill Drive, Suite G
University of Utah
Salt Lake City, Utah 84109
AC 801-581-6281
FTS 524-5500
Marie Roane, Project Officer

States served:
Nevada, Utah,
Colorado, Arizona,
New Mexico, BIA Schools

REGIONAL RESOURCE CENTERS (continued)

Mid-West Regional Resource Center
Dr. Raymond Feltner, Director
Drake University
1332-26th Street
Des Moines, Iowa 50311
AC 515-271-3936
FTS 862-4737
Etta J. Waugh, Project Officer

States served:
North Dakota, Oklahoma,
South Dakota,
Nebraska, Kansas,
Missouri, Arkansas

Mid-East Regional Resource Center
Dr. Raymond Cottrell, Director
George Washington University
1901 Pennsylvania Avenue, N.W.
Suite 505
Washington, D.C. 20006
AC 202-676-7200
FTS 254-3700
Etta J. Waugh, Project Officer

States served:
Maryland, Delaware,
West Virginia,
North Carolina

Mid-South Regional Resource Center
Mr. Robert Sterrett, Director
University of Kentucky Research Foundation
Porter Building, Room 131
Lexington, Kentucky 40506
AC 606-258-4921
FTS 355-2781 or 355-2644 or 2645
Etta J. Waugh, Project Officer

States served:
Kentucky, Tennessee,
Virginia

District of Columbia Regional Resource Center
Dr. Rosa Trapp-Duke
Howard University
2935 Upton Street, N.W.
Washington, D.C. 20008
AC 202-686-6729
Etta J. Waugh, Project Officer

States served:
District of Columbia

Southeast Regional Resource Center
Dr. Faye Brown, Director
Auburn University at Montgomery
Montgomery, Alabama 36117
AC 205-279-9110 Ext. 442
FTS 534-7515
Marie Roane, Project Officer

States served:
Louisiana, Mississippi,
Alabama, Georgia,
South Carolina,
Florida, Puerto Rico,
Virgin Islands

REGIONAL RESOURCE CENTERS (continued)

Pennsylvania Regional Resource Center
Dr. Jim Duffey, Director
Pennsylvania State Department of Education
500 Valley Forge Plaza
1150 First Avenue
King of Prussia, Pennsylvania 19406
AC 215-265-3706
FTS 596-1430
Marie Roane, Project Officer

States served:
Pennsylvania

Illinois Regional Resource Center
Dr. Gaylan Kapperman, Director
Northern Illinois University
Graham Hall 243
DeKalb, Illinois 60115
AC 815-753-0534
Marine Roane, Project Officer

States served:
Illinois

Northeast Regional Resource Center
Dr. Nicholas J. Maldari, Director
New Jersey State Department of Education
168 Bank Street
Hightstown, New Jersey 08520
AC 609-448-4773
FTS 483-2311 or 483-2214
Etta J. Waugh, Project Officer

States served:
Maine, Vermont,
New Hampshire,
Massachusetts,
Rhode Island,
Connecticut,
New Jersey

New York State Regional Resource Center
Dr. Lee Cummings, Director
New York State Education Department
55 Elk Street
Albany, New York 12234
AC 518-474-2251
FTS 472-7366
Marie Roane, Project Officer

States served:
New York

New York City Regional Resource Center
Mr. Martin Hayott, Director
City University of New York
33 West 42nd Street
New York, New York 10036
AC 212-790-4797 or 4407 or 4408
Marie Roane, Project Officer

States served:
New York City only

REGIONAL RESOURCE CENTERS (continued)

Leroy V. Goodman, Director
Division of Media Services
Bureau of Education for the Handicapped
U.S. Office of Education
400 Maryland Avenue, S.W. DONO 4853
Washington, D.C. 20202
Telephone: (202) 472-1494

When choosing any material, the considerations should be the same for the exceptional children as they are for the other children in your room. Is the material appropriate to the needs of the children? Following are some questions that you should ask yourself when choosing a material, no matter if it is borrowed from the instructional materials center or if you are considering purchasing such materials.

QUESTIONS TO ASK WHEN CONSIDERING INSTRUCTIONAL MATERIAL

Considerations Regarding the Physical Characteristics and Content

1. Is the material constructed and packaged well enough for classroom use?
2. Is the appearance of the material appealing and the content interesting?
3. Is the material safe?
4. Is the material durable?
5. Is the content current and accurate?
6. Are the instructions clear?
7. Are the concepts clearly presented?

Questions Covering the Cost and Use of the Material

1. Can the instructional objectives be attained as effectively by less expensive means?
2. Can the material be used to accomplish a number of different objectives over time?
3. Will unreasonable demands be made on your time in order for the students to use the material?
4. Will additional equipment or supplies be needed to utilize the materials effectively?
5. Is part of the package consumable?
6. Can the students use this material independently?
7. How many children can participate at one time?
8. Is the material teacher directed or student directed?
9. Will the material fit your existing storage space?

Some Questions Relating to the Students

1. Do the requirements for using the material match your student's physical and mental needs?
2. What range of abilities does the material cover?
3. Does use of the material require additional skills, personal characteristics, or physical responses which would be inconsistent with your students' level of development?
4. Does the material encourage a student to participate actively?
5. Will the children participate as individuals or as a group?

Considerations Pertaining to Your Instructional and Curriculum Objectives

1. Are there objectives stated for the use of the material?
2. Is this material suitable to your curriculum and to your objectives?
3. Does this material allow adequate practice of your targeted skill?
4. Is the amount of time required to use this material in keeping with your overall curriculum objectives?
5. Is there a sequence in the material that proceeds from simple to complex, in small steps and logical order?
6. Can you adapt the materials for your assessment and teaching objectives?
7. Is the material self-correcting?
8. Can you establish a feedback procedure for the material?
9. Will there be an easy transition to subsequent materials?

Questions to Ask Yourself When Considering Toys for Classroom Use

1. Is the toy of good quality material, sturdy, and well built?
2. Are there any loose or protruding nails?
3. Are the wooden toy corners rounded and finished so as to prevent splinters?
4. Does the toy have any openings which might catch a child's fingers?
5. Are paints used lead-free, nonpoisonous and resistant to chipping or peeling?
6. Is there hard enamel with a varnish coating that will furnish a durable surface for toys that need frequent washing?
7. Are the decorations large enough so that they cannot fit into the nose, mouth, or ears?
8. Is the toy easy to handle and easy to grasp?
9. Is the toy able to be sterilized and washed easily? (Rather than painstakingly washing each individual toy used by young children, placing several in a net bag and dipping them in a bucket of bleach solution is usually adequate for classroom sterilization purposes. The bag can be hung by its strings to dry. Can the toy withstand this treatment?)
10. Is the handle on a push toy protected with a large knob or bar?
11. Have you read the contents on any toy such as clay or paint to see if dangerous ingredients are used?

Certainly, to be appropriate, the materials must match the needs of the children for whom they are intended. In the initial acquisition stage, we want to know if the material is for matching, for cognition, or for recall. Each level requires more learning on the part of the children, and we want to make sure that the children are at the level that the material requires before we assign their use. Otherwise, we are apt to frustrate the children and turn them against learning, when materials at a lower level would enable them to experience success.

Sometimes we do not have materials available that allow the children to function at their current levels. In such a case, it may be necessary to alter the procedures that are normally used with the materials, or it may be essential to reduce the content of the material. For example, the sequence puzzles that are often used may be too lengthy and have too many steps for the children who are going to be using them. Instead of ordering simpler materials that may come a long time after you have use for them, it can be a simple adaptation to reduce the content by removing part of the pictures. Putting in the beginning picture, the middle, and the end will be all that some children may be able to process. As they become more proficient, however, you can add more steps and help them to see a complete sequence.

Homemade materials can also be of help. Polaroid pictures of a trip that the children have taken can be used on the spot to show a sequence. For some children, the sequence may show them getting on the bus to leave school, a picture of the place visited, and a picture getting off the bus. For other children, there may be the complete sequence of getting on the bus, events during the ride, the arrival at the place visited, various things that took place during the visit, getting back on the bus, events during the ride home, and the arrival back at school. The level of materials is always determined by the level of functioning of the children who are to use the materials.

THE ERIC SYSTEM

Information regarding particular subject matter can be found indexed under the Educational Resources Information Center (ERIC). These indexes can be found in many educational libraries. ERIC is a nationwide, comprehensive information system designed to serve American education. The ERIC system is responsible for making available to the public the findings of research in education. ERIC currently includes 16 decentralized clearinghouses, each focused on a separate subject matter area. These clearinghouses and the subject matter for which they are responsible are as follows:

1. Adult, Career and Vocational Education
   Ohio State University
   1960 Kenny Road
   Columbus, Ohio, 43210

2. Counseling and Personnel Services
   University of Michigan
   School of Education Building, Room 2108
   East University and South University Streets
   Ann Arbor, Michigan 48109

3. Educational Management
   University of Oregon
   Eugene, Oregon 97403

4. Elementary and Early Childhood Education
   University of Illinois
   College of Education
   Urbana, Illinois 61801

5. Handicapped and Gifted Children
   1920 Association Drive
   Reston, Virginia 22091

6. Higher Education
   George Washington University
   One Dupont Circle, N.W., Suite 630
   Washington, D.C. 20036

7. Information Resources
   Syracuse University
   School of Education
   Syracuse, New York 13210

8. Junior Colleges
   University of California at Los Angeles
   Powell Library, Room 96
   405 Hilgard Avenue
   Los Angeles, California 90024

9. Languages and Linguistics
   Center for Applied Linguistics
   1611 North Kent Street
   Arlington, Virginia 22209

10. Reading and Communication Skills
    National Council of Teachers of English
    111 Kenyon Road
    Urbana, Illinois 61801

11. Rural Education and Small Schools
    New Mexico State University
    Box 3AP
    Las Cruces, New Mexico 88003

12. Science, Mathematics, and Environmental Education
    Ohio State University
    1200 Chambers Rd., 3rd Flr.
    Columbus, Ohio 43212

13. Social Studies/Social Science Education
    855 Broadway
    Boulder, Colorado 80302

14. Teacher Education
    American Association of Colleges for Teacher Education
    One Dupont Circle, Suite 616
    Washington, D.C. 20036

15. Tests, Measurement, and Evaluation
    Educational Testing Service
    Princeton, New Jersey 08541

16. Urban Education
    Columbia University, Teachers College
    Box 40
    New York, New York 10027

Sometimes you will need additional information about the type of handicapping conditions that some of the children are demonstrating. Most types of handicapping conditions have a national organization that is available for information about that specific handicapping condition. Below are some of the national organizations with their addresses that were current at the time of this writing. Often there are local chapters of these national organizations that can give you information about the local efforts of dealing with that type of handicapped children. These organizations are usually listed in the phone book or may be in the directory of community services available in your region. By contacting them, you can receive information about dealing with the children. Most of the organizations now have low cost material with information for the teacher of mainstreamed children. Parents are often another source that you can use to obtain information regarding the various types of handicapping conditions. Perhaps they will share information with you that they have found particularly helpful.

PARTIAL LIST OF AGENCIES SERVING THE HANDICAPPED

Alexander Graham Bell Association for the Deaf
  The Volta Bureau
  3417 Volta Place, NW
  Washington, D.C. 20007

Professional organization; publishes *Volta Review* and serves as clearing-house for information on the deaf.

American Diabetes Association
  18 E. 48th St.
  New York, New York 10017

Information regarding childhood diabetes.

Association for Education of the Visually Handicapped
  919 Walnut St., 4th Floor
  Philadelphia, Pennsylvania 19107

Professional organization; publications: *Education of the Visually Handicapped, Fountainhead;* information on visually handicapped.

American Foundation for the Blind
  15 West 16th Street
  New York, New York 10011

Publications on visual handicaps, *Braille and Talking Book Review;* produces educational aids that can be used by blind and low-vision people. Free list of publications and materials available.

American Hearing Society
  919 88th Street, NW
  Washington, D.C. 20006

Promotes "Better Hearing Month" and publishes pamphlets, *Hearing News* and *AHS Bulletin Board.*

American Heart Association, Inc.
  44 East 23rd Street
  New York, New York 10010

Information regarding heart problems.

American Printing House for the Blind
  1839 Frankfort Avenue
  P.O. Box 6085
  Louisville, Kentucky 40206

Publications: catalogs of braille, large-type and talking books, educational tape recordings, tangible apparatus, braille music, and numerous periodicals in both braille and talking book format.

American Speech-Language-Hearing Association
    9030 Old Georgetown Road
    Washington, D.C. 20014

Professional Organization, Publishes: *Journal of Speech and Hearing Disorders, Journal of Speech and Hearing Research,* and *ASHA.*

Arthritis Foundation
    1213 Avenue of the Americas
    New York, New York 20036

Information regarding arthritis.

Association for Children with Learning Disabilities (ACLD)
    4156 Library Road
    Pittsburgh, Pennsylvania 15234

Information on children with learning disabilities.

Convention of American Instructors of the Deaf
    5034 Wisconsin Avenue, NW
    Washington, D.C. 20016

Professional organization; publication: *American Annals of the Deaf;* information on deafness.

Council for Exceptional Children
    1920 Association Drive
    Reston, Virginia 22091

Professional organization; publications: *Exceptional Children, Teaching Exceptional Children, Update;* information regarding exceptional children.

Division for the Blind and Physically Handicapped
    Library of Congress
    Washington, D.C. 20542

Local and/or state libraries. Supplies magazines and books in braille, talking books, and machines, records, and writing and listening appliances for the blind and physically handicapped.

Epilepsy Foundation
    Suite 406, 1828 L Street, NW
    Washington, D.C. 20036

Information regarding epilepsy.

League for Emotionally Disturbed Children
    171 Madison Avenue
    New York, New York 10017

Information regarding emotional disturbance.

Media Services and Captioned Films Branch
    Division of Educational Services
    U.S. Office of Education
    Washington, D.C. 20202

Information on captioned films for deaf distributed through regional offices.

Muscular Dystrophy Associations of America
    810 Seventh Avenue
    New York, New York 10019

Information regarding muscular dystrophy.

National Association for Mental Health, Inc.
    1800 North Kent Street
    Arlington, Virginia 22209

Information regarding mental health.

National Association for Retarded Citizens
    2709 Avenue E East
    P.O. Box 6109
    Arlington, Texas 76011

Information and advocacy regarding mentally retarded.

National Center on Child Abuse
    Office of Child Development
    P.O. Box 1182
    Washington, D.C. 20013

Information regarding child abuse.

National Easter Seal Society for Crippled Children and Adults, Inc.
    2023 W. Ogden Avenue
    Chicago, Illinois 60612

Information regarding all types of crippling conditions.

National Foundation/March of Dimes
  1275 Mammroneck Avenue
  White Plains, New York 10605

Information regarding birth defects.

National Multiple Sclerosis Society
  257 Park Avenue South
  New York, New York 10010

Information regarding multiple sclerosis.

National Society for Autistic Children
  306 31st St.
  Huntington, West Virginia 25702

Information and referral service regarding autism.

National Society for the Prevention of Blindness
  78 Madison Avenue
  New York, New York 10016

Publications: *Sight Saving Review, Wise Owl, Newsletter,* pamphlets, reprints of journal articles. Information about vision.

United Cerebral Palsy Associations, Inc.
  66 East 34th Street
  New York, New York 10016

Information regarding cerebral palsy.

In summary, you as a teacher working with special children can decide that a problem exists by looking at the assessment procedures you've used with the children. By examining the children, the task, and the setting, you can determine *where* the problem exists. After deciding what the problem is and where it is, you then must establish the teaching objective, the criterion that the children must meet, and follow with the development of your educational plan. Once these things are done, you must implement the teaching strategies.

Then comes the hardest part of all, for it often tests a teacher's endurance and commitment to teaching. You must teach and test to see if the children have learned what was taught. If not, you must revise the material, teach it, and again test to see if the revised material was learned. If not, you must break down the task even further, revise the material, and teach again, testing to see if the material was learned. Only through such continuous assessment can you determine if the material is being learned and the objectives met.

Only through such methods will you know for sure that the special children within your room are receiving the kind of education that will help them become the type of persons that they are capable of becoming. It's not easy. No one ever said it would be. Most children learn, no matter how badly we teach or what we teach. Most exceptional children don't. Exceptional children have to be well taught. Their success illustrates yours. Good luck to you!

INDEX